Online Teaching

Online Teaching

Tools and Techniques to Achieve Success with Learners

Mike Casey, Erin Shaw,
Jeff Whittingham, and
Nancy Gallavan

ROWMAN & LITTLEFIELD
Lanham • Boulder • New York • London

Published by Rowman & Littlefield
An imprint of The Rowman & Littlefield Publishing Group, Inc.
4501 Forbes Boulevard, Suite 200, Lanham, Maryland 20706
www.rowman.com

Unit A, Whitacre Mews, 26–34 Stannary Street, London SE11 4AB

British Library Cataloguing in Publication Information Available

Library of Congress Cataloging-in-Publication Data

Names: Casey, K. Michael, author. | Shaw, Erin, author. | Whittingham, Jeff, author. | Gallavan, Nancy P., author.
Title: Online teaching : tools and techniques to achieve success with learners / Mike Casey, Erin Shaw, Jeff Whittingham, and Nancy Gallavan.
Description: Lanham, Maryland : Rowman & Littlefield, [2018]
Identifiers: LCCN 2018015085 (print) | LCCN 2018019663 (ebook) | ISBN 9781475839371 (electronic) | ISBN 9781475839357 (cloth : alk. paper) | ISBN 9781475839364 (pbk. : alk. paper)
Subjects: LCSH: Web-based instruction—Study and teaching. | Educational technology—Study and teaching. | Education, Higher—Computer-assisted instruction.
Classification: LCC LB1044.87 (ebook) | LCC LB1044.87 .C38 2018 (print) | DDC 371.33/44678—dc23
LC record available at https://lccn.loc.gov/2018015085

Contents

Preface

Online education has grown at an ever-increasing rate since the internet gained wide access in the early 1990s. Since that time, instructors have worked to make the transition from face-to-face to online instruction. Some have done it successfully and others have struggled. While universities were the first to harness the internet as an access point for students, online education is now available at the high school level as well as in the corporate world.

No matter the purpose for online instruction, there has and will continue to be a need for high-quality instruction for online teachers. This is true of the beginning, novice, and more experienced online teacher alike. It is important to realize that good teaching is good teaching whether in a physical classroom or in one of many online formats. This book seeks to direct online teachers to those practices that represent good teaching.

The primary purpose of this book is to provide practical advice for beginning and novice online instructors who wish to establish and enhance their online teaching and improve online learning for their students. However, the best practices described here may also be of use by more experienced educators seeking to revitalize their online teaching. The book is meant to be an accessible reference for improving online teaching and learning regardless of teaching background.

There are few greater challenges for a teacher than developing and teaching your first online course. Even the most excellent traditional classroom teachers can feel overwhelmed by this task. This book will give you the tools and techniques necessary to meet the challenge of achieving success with your online learners.

Chapter 1

Online Teaching and Learning

How This Book Will Help You Become a Better Online Instructor

Dr. John Michaels was feeling positive about his first year of teaching in higher education. As a former junior high language arts teacher, he had been able to make a relatively smooth transition into the literacy education program at a nearby university. As he was sitting in his office on the last day of finals week he reflected, "No matter what level, teaching is teaching." At the height of his feelings of personal gratification, his department chair stepped into his office.

It wasn't long before John's elation transformed into severe anxiety. His department chair informed him that there was a new section of Literacy across the Curriculum that needed to be developed and taught online the next fall. John had never considered teaching an online class; now he would be responsible for one in just a few short months, and he did not know where to begin.

WHAT IS ONLINE TEACHING AND LEARNING?

Online teaching and learning is education that takes place through the internet. It can be divided into two categories: synchronous and asynchronous. *Synchronous instruction* is defined as instruction and learning that occurs in real time via the internet, while *asynchronous instruction* and learning occurs at any time via the internet. One is not better than the other. Instructors determine which type of instruction best fits their teaching methodologies and teaching style.

There are advantages and disadvantages to every endeavor, and online teaching is no different. One of the primary advantages of online teaching is the student-centered nature of online teaching. While students may attend a face-to-face class and leave with only minimal interaction, online learning

1

requires active participation in the learning process, both with fellow students and with the professor. It is possible for students to attend a face-to-face class for an entire semester and choose to not interact with the instructor. That is rarely possible in an effectively structured online environment.

Online instructors make contact with each student through e-mail, and many join in chats and discussions in which all students are expected to participate. This student-centered focus also promotes collaboration. Students must interact with the other students, either in whole group activities or in small groups. The strong collaborative component of online learning tends to create a positive experience for students and provides a connection for the course that can be lost in the traditional classroom.

Online learning also allows for greater accessibility, removing geographical barriers to education. This is true of high school courses offered to remote locations, out-of-state programs in areas where they are not offered locally, and corporate training sessions involving sites around the world. Many universities reach more diverse populations than is possible in the traditional setting.

Greater flexibility and convenience is also an important feature of online learning. This is especially true for nontraditional learners who have full-time employment that hinders their ability to pursue education in any other way. Online learning also allows students to learn from their own homes, in a comfortable setting, with no traveling.

Along with the advantages of online teaching and learning come a few disadvantages. Some novice online instructors have a great fear of online teaching. This fear may stem from unfamiliarity with the technological tools and skills necessary to teach online. Many also fear that online teaching reduces the rigor of the course and overcompensate by creating an unrealistic workload for students.

Other online instructors struggle to develop a sense of personal presence in the online classroom, which keeps them from building a true learning community. For many of these instructors, the shift from being the center of the classroom into the position of facilitator can be daunting. This book seeks to eliminate the fear associated with online teaching and remove these perceived disadvantages.

HOW THIS BOOK IS ORGANIZED

Chapter 2: Foundations and Formats of Online Teaching and Learning

Chapter 2 expands on the foundations and formats available to today's online teacher. This chapter begins by describing the extraordinary benefits of online teaching and then discusses the possible pitfalls associated with online teaching and learning. The chapter also describes online pedagogy, delivery formats, and key concepts and vocabulary.

Chapter 2 provides crucial information for any novice online instructor because it will help familiarize you with the basic principles of online teaching and learning. This chapter should be read before reading any other chapter if you are new to online teaching.

Tools, Techniques, and Tips

Following chapter 2, the next six chapters focus on the major aspects of course development and design. After reading and understanding the foundations and formats, you will be able to use these chapters in the order that they are most relevant to you. These chapters can be read in sequential order or as stand-alone references for building and improving elements of your course.

Each of these chapters consists of the following three parts:

1. Tools for Online Teaching
   - In the tools section of each chapter you will discover the most relevant and available tools that apply to the chapter content. The tools in these sections include learning management system functions, web 2.0 tools, and online-appropriate assignment types.
2. Techniques for Online Teaching
   - In the techniques section of each chapter you will be able to equip yourself with proven techniques for developing and improving your online course. The techniques found here have been successfully implemented by many online instructors and should have a home in any effective teacher's course.
3. Tips for Online Teaching
   - In the tips section of each chapter we have summarized, created, and curated many beneficial approaches to improving your online course. These tips are meant to help you quickly solve many of the most common difficulties that novice online instructors encounter.

Chapter 3: Course Organization and Learning Management

Chapter 3 describes course organization and learning management for online instruction. This content in this chapter is vital, as it will equip novice online instructors with the ability to develop courses with student learning in mind. Developing a new online course can be an intimidating task, and this chapter will help mitigate many common uncertainties faced by new course developers.

Chapter 4: Building Community and Effective Communication

Chapter 4 discusses building community and implementing effective communication techniques. The chapter focuses on helping novice online instructors to close the gap between themselves and their students. For many online instructors the lack of physical immediacy can be an obstacle to effectively communicating with students.

The absence of an active learning community can also have a detrimental effect on student engagement and performance. Chapter 4 tackles this issue, providing practical tools, techniques, and tips that enhance communication between instructor and students. Implementing these approaches will ensure that you address this common complaint associated with teaching and taking an online course.

Chapter 5: Course Layout and Instructional Design

Chapter 5 explores course layout and instructional design. This chapter describes best practices for designing a visually engaging and accessible online course. Effective online instructors implement design strategies that promote learning through the way course content is displayed.

It is the instructor's responsibility to ensure inclusion for all learners, regardless of ability. Accessibility is an important issue in education, and the instructor must maintain a learning environment that is accessible to all students, including those with physical and learning disabilities. Creating an accessible course benefits not only learners with disabilities, but every student in the course. The tips, techniques, and tools in this chapter will equip you to design such a course.

Chapter 6: Course Information and Learner Support

Chapter 6 delves into course information and learner support strategies. This chapter explains the importance of providing students with support resources that can be accessed at any time. Online students are faced with the difficult task of learning how to find, complete, and submit all of their assignments each time they begin a new online course. This learning curve is often lessened or heightened by the instructor's practices.

Prepared students will explore the course and ask questions, while other students will spend countless hours confused about different aspects of the course. The tools, techniques, and tips in this chapter will show you how to create a repository of course resources and course orientation materials to decrease the learning curve for your students, allowing them to begin learning the course content sooner.

Chapter 7: Course Goals and Performance Assessments

Chapter 7 introduces you to the processes of writing course goals based on academic and assessment standards to frame your online course, aligning the curriculum and instruction with the goals and the assessments, and developing assessments to be conducted when following the assessment cycle. Chapter 7 provides tools, techniques, and tips for constructing assessments to increase student engagement and achievement, with attention to the methods of expression, levels of thinking, and forms of assessment and including insights for creating checklists, writing rubrics, and using mobile technology.

Chapter 8: Data Analysis and Course Improvement

Finally, chapter 8 provides guidance in modifying and improving online teaching. This chapter details the necessary steps for recording outcomes, analyzing data, and interpreting findings in order to observe each student's progress and change over time with graphs as well as to examine each assessment item for its effectiveness.

This chapter describes six parts of the online course that impact your course assessments and data analysis, including ways to increase student learning and enhance teacher efficacy. Toward the end of each semester it becomes vitally important to analyze your course with an eye toward improving it for the following semester. The tools, techniques, and tips in this chapter will give you the necessary strategies to maintain continuous improvement.

PREPARE FOR SUCCESS

The best advice for the beginning or novice online teacher is to prepare for success. This preparation takes many forms, but it begins with an open mind. Instructors should prepare for the online classroom by being organized and building structure into their online classrooms. Online instructors should hold the same high expectations for their online students as they do for traditional students.

Online teachers should also seek support from any source. With explicit planning and organization and with a support structure in place, traditional teachers can be successful online instructors. This book is designed to provide those important support structures for the novice online teacher and to provide a vast repository of tools, techniques, and tips that any online teacher will find beneficial.

Chapter 2

Foundations and Formats of Online Teaching and Learning

Exploring the Extraordinary Benefits and Possible Pitfalls of Online Teaching and Learning

Dr. John Mckay had finally decided to begin the arduous task of converting his American Nations I course to an online format. Recently, his university had been incentivizing instructors who were developing online courses, and John knew that he needed to "get with the times," as his colleagues had put it, but he honestly didn't know how to begin. He stared blankly at his computer screen and realized that he should probably log into his faculty account on the university home page.

John had heard other faculty use terms like learning management system, Blackboard, *and* synchronous instruction, *but he knew he was ignorant of their application to online learning. The only thing that John knew for sure was that he had more questions than answers. The worst part was that he really didn't have an idea of who to ask for help. He was afraid asking someone in his department would make him look foolish, so he picked up the phone and dialed the information technology division; maybe they could point him in the right direction.*

Online courses have been around since 1989 when the University of Phoenix became one of the first institutions to offer courses over the internet. Online learning, sometimes referred to as *eLearning*, is taking teaching and learning outside of the traditional brick-and-mortar environment and into virtual spaces utilizing the World Wide Web.

Online education is a different method of teaching and learning compared to to traditional face-to-face methods, and therefore requires a different pedagogy and overall structure. Since the mid-1990s, online instruction has soared to include institutions from K–12 to postsecondary levels across the United States that offer online teaching and learning opportunities to students of all ages. Due to the diversity in age levels and the content that can be provided, there are a multitude of foundations that support online learning and a variety of formats for delivery of instruction.

FOUNDATIONS OF ONLINE TEACHING AND LEARNING

Online teaching and learning offers many benefits that provide the foundations of online instruction. There also barriers that can cause challenges that erode online instruction. Foundations include active engagement, differentiation, and convenience, while the most common barriers include difficulty in building rapport and relationships within the online course, difficulty in determining ways to increase online discussion and interaction between the students and the instructor, and accessibility issues.

Active Engagement

One major advantage of online education is the propensity to offer a more active learning environment than can be found in traditional face-to-face courses. Online courses are often designed based on a constructivist theory of instruction, where the learning is more active rather than passive in nature. The constructivist theory allows the instructor to serve as a facilitator to provide scaffolding of content for the learners, but the learning is actively enhanced through an in-depth exploration of the content by the learner.

Within online course instruction, content can be offered using tools that allow learners to progress at their own pace. Content can be revisited when needed. Strategies for incorporating active learning into online courses include:

* well-conceived discussion prompts that invite discourse
* synchronous online meetings
* cooperative group work
* performance-based adaptive assessments that allow the learner to demonstrate understanding of content
* virtual interactions
* problem-based learning assignments

Convenience

In addition to providing an active learning environment, online education also offers convenience. Online education allows materials to be presented any time and in any location where students have access to the internet, and online materials can be updated so that learners see the changes immediately.

Location and distance are not issues for the instructor or the learner, and asynchronous online learning is not hindered by time zones. Online learning facilitates *situated learning*, or the application of knowledge and skills in specific contexts, since learners can complete online courses while working on the job or in their own space and can contextualize the learning at their own pace.

Differentiation

The nature of online learning is to offer content in a variety of delivery methods to meet the learning needs of different learning styles—kinesthetic, auditory, and visual. In an online learning environment, online learning tools and activities can be utilized to determine individual learners' needs and current levels of expertise, and then to assign appropriate materials for learners to select from in order to achieve their desired learning outcomes.

There are a variety of strategies for offering content that help with differentiation. Text-based reading in the form of textbooks (print or digital), journal articles, and blogs can deliver relevant content easily. Another strategy is to include videos that offer either informational content or lectures in the form of a screencast of a PowerPoint or some other presentation tool. Podcasts can be used to deliver audio content, and demonstrations can be a useful tool to demonstrate processes specific to certain content areas. Additionally, simulations can be used to reinforce student learning in real-world contexts. A similar strategy would be to offer content through a game format, which can sometimes be more engaging and less stressful than a simulation.

Possible Pitfalls of Online Teaching and Learning

One of the most common challenges in online learning is building rapport and relationships among course participants. The nature of online instruction does not offer the same personal interaction as one would find in a face-to-face class. Often communication is unidirectional, either through text (where tone can be misinterpreted or seem flat) or through video or audio content (where the instructor introduces him- or herself and/or introduces content). This can lead to a decrease in interaction between instructor and students and even less interaction among the students.

Depending on the structure of the online course, there may be difficulty in determining ways to increase online discussion and interaction between the students and the instructor. Therefore, additional planning needs to occur prior to the beginning of an online course to establish connections, both between instructor and students and among the students.

An additional challenge is student accessibility, which could be caused by a disability or as a result of technological issues. The course material's accessibility may be limited if a learner has a disability such as a hearing impairment or visual impairment, which creates a need to provide an alternate access to videos or podcasts in the form of closed-captioning and/or screen-reading software.

Technological issues may also affect online teaching and learning. These issues may be insufficient bandwidth and internet connectivity issues, which create a problematic learning experience because they create difficulty in accessing course material and possibly cause learners to lag behind their virtual classmates. Another technical challenge may include the computer skills of the learners. While many learners are tech savvy in this digital age, online learning management systems may pose challenges in terms of browser compatibility issues or content delivery structures that learners may not know how to navigate.

FORMATS OF ONLINE TEACHING AND LEARNING

Online software platforms offer a variety of formats for housing online instruction. While sometimes thought to be interchangeable terms, *learning management system* (LMS) and *learning content management system* (LCMS) platforms, although they share a few functionalities, are very different in reality.

Learning Management Systems

Learning management systems are software applications that allow companies, schools, and other organizations to administer, document, track, and report on the delivery of online courses and training programs. An LMS delivers learning content and tracks course access, completions, and test scores; however, it is not used to create content. The main function is for the management online content. Some common free learning management systems and their best features include:

Schoology
- free for individuals
- rubrics, standards alignment, and web-based grading available

- user-friendly for learners and instructors
- supports the Learning Tools Interoperability (LTI) standard
- gamification features (including custom badges) and allows instant messaging

Moodle (Modular Object-Oriented Dynamic Learning Environment)
- available as a limited free version or full feature paid version
- open-source initiative that can be customized or modified through modular plugins that allow instructors to add or create features as needed
- supports activities such as peer assessments, real-time messaging, and wiki forums
- provides progress tracking and reporting options

Edmodo
- free to use
- social media–style interface with a messaging feature
- contains learner, instructor, and parent views
- useful third-party integrations available
- integrates with most popular K–12 school student information systems
- spotlight feature makes sharing resources simple
- offers Common Core microassessments
- does not support the LTI standard

Google Classroom
- included with Google's education institution license
- does not have a grade book, well-defined roles, or advanced reporting
- does not support LTI, through which instructors might connect Classroom to existing LMS or student information systems (SIS); instead utilizes the ubiquity of G Suite for Education to offer a simple online complement to in-person classes
- provides an easy way for educators who are already using Google products (including Google Docs, Sheets, and Slides, and Google Hangouts) to experiment with online learning

Learning Content Management Systems

Learning content management systems are tools for actually creating learning content, publishing that content in a variety of formats, and delivering the content. An LCMS can be used to develop content using design templates, allowing the reuse of content elements across a course, importing and integrating content from other authoring tools, and publishing the content to multiple outputs and devices.

Learning content management systems differ from learning management systems in the ways mentioned; however, going forward in this book the term *learning management system* will be used to refer to both LMS and LCMS. The two most common learning classroom management systems are Blackboard and Canvas by Instructure. Here are some of their available features:

Blackboard
- price determined by the institution
- the most popular educational LCMS; used by many institutions
- third-party partners with many academic publishers develop and enable a wide range of electronic text and content to integrate with Blackboard
- an extensive list of educational tools and services including, but not limited to:
  - announcements
  - calendar
  - tasks
  - grade book
  - course messages
  - blogs
  - wikis
  - journals
  - discussion
  - content pages, folders, modules

Canvas by Instructure
- available as a free version; paid version has more tools and features and is priced slightly more competitively than Blackboard
- an extensive list of educational tools and services including, but not limited to:
  - announcements feature
  - calendar
  - tasks
  - grade book
  - course messages
  - blogs
  - wikis
  - journals
  - discussion
  - content pages, folders, modules
- some major features offered are web hosting and extensive third-party integrations with a variety of supplementary tools and services, including:

- from within the built-in grade book, instructors can launch SpeedGrader to access submissions alongside preconfigured learning outcomes and rubrics
- instructors can preview and annotate submissions within the browser, so they don't need to download any files
- Microsoft Office, Google Docs, and PDFs are all visible on Canvas
- in addition to text-based feedback, instructors can add inline annotations, such as highlights, text strikeouts, and freehand drawings
- when the peer review feature is enabled, all annotation tools are available to learners as well

SYNCHRONOUS AND ASYNCHRONOUS DELIVERY

As discussed in chapter 1, the two major formats for delivery of online teaching and learning are asynchronous online learning, where students can access the online materials at any time, synchronous online learning, which allows for real-time interaction between students and instructors. A third format, called *blended instruction*, includes elements of both synchronous and asynchronous instruction.

Synchronous Instruction

With synchronous online instruction, learners and the instructor are in an LMS in real time for delivery of material and information. Synchronous instruction is the online method most similar to a traditional face-to-face classroom, and instructors adopt tools and online instructional methods that support real-time learning and discussion.

Technology matters when it comes to online instruction. Instructional methods both depend on and inform how and when content is delivered. When teaching large classes, instructors may find tools that allow student-audio to interrupt lectures disruptive, and those that allow live two-way video (at will) impractical for a large audience.

An alternative might be to include technologies that allow instructors to maintain audio and video control while giving students a chance to ask questions and engage in discussion using a live chat feature. A class discussion board provides another more structured means of addressing questions and discussions learners may have. Small classes, however, can often accommodate live two-way audio and video, which serves to provide a more personal, classroom-like learning experience.

Instructors who teach synchronous courses are not limited to just one content delivery method; instead, they can combine methods with additional technologies to accommodate a wide range of learners. The following tools are just some of those that support real-time communication:

• video-streaming platforms
• web-conferencing tools
• live chats
• telephone availability
• virtual office hours

Each of these tools encourages live participation and interaction. With most learning management systems, instructors are able to capture and upload lecture videos and chat transcripts for learners to access in the event of an absence.

Asynchronous Instruction

Asynchronous instruction gives instructors the opportunity to provide materials and information via online tools that allow learners to view lectures, access materials and information, and collaborate with instructors and peers on their own schedule. Lectures might be prerecorded or presented on screencast software or PowerPoint with an instructor voiceover. These delivery methods allow students to review and access content as necessary.

Courses that use asynchronous content delivery methods require a different approach to teaching—one that depends heavily upon the technologies used. As with synchronous instruction, characteristics such as class size and instructor preferences can influence which tools are used in asynchronous online classes. More than one technology is typically employed to deliver content effectively, and instructors who use an asynchronous format often pull from a large instructional toolbox to ensure multiple opportunities to access content. Some of the technology tools include the following:

• downloadable prerecorded lectures
• Microsoft PowerPoint presentations, with or without voiceover
• forums and discussion boards
• e-mail communication
• Google Drive and similar collaborative tools
• tools for off-hours support, including virtual tutoring centers and virtual resource centers

Each of these delivery formats allows instructors to overcome teaching challenges associated with not being in the LMS at the same time as the learners.

Blended Instruction

Blended instruction involves the instructor and learners working together using mixed delivery modes. Instruction incorporates several typical online face-to-face activities along with technology-mediated activities. This allows instructors to provide learning outcomes that are pedagogically supported through assignments, activities, and assessments as appropriate for a given content sequence and that bridge synchronous delivery with asynchronous delivery of content and information in a manner meaningful to the learner.

Tips for Ensuring Best Format Selection

- Know your learners.
  - Synchronous courses work best when learners need the most scaffolding and are not self-motivated.
  - Asynchronous courses work best when learners have many outside responsibilities (a full-time job and/or family) and when the learners are self-motivated.
  - Blended courses work best when scaffolding of content needs to be offered directly from the instructor but allows learners to continue at their own pace.
- Develop learning goals.
  - Begin with the end in mind to help determine whether a synchronous, asynchronous or blended format will work best.
  - Ask yourself: What are the key concepts and/or skills students need to master by the end of the course? The answer to this question will help in developing course content, activities, and assessments that align with your learning goals, as well as in choosing the appropriate technology for delivery of content.

Chapter 3

Course Organization and Learning Management

Developing a Course with Student Learning in Mind

Professor Lakynn Mason was considering the upcoming presentation as-signment in her traditional face-to-face business ethics course. She loved the way that the students responded to their assignment to analyze a specific business case and work with two classmates to develop a three-sided story of the events. Each student was required to assume a role within the case and to defend his or her position. Lakynn's students became animated defending their positions, often remarking on how they never considered the gray area in each situation.

Lakynn also thought that it would be a wonderful addition to her online section of the same course, but it was a daunting task. Even if she wanted to try to implement such an assignment, she did not know where to start. The project would lose its strength without the case aspect, the group aspect, or the presentation aspect; those were all things that she did not know how to accomplish in the online setting individually—and especially not all at once.

COURSE ORGANIZATION AND LEARNING MANAGEMENT

Course organization, as it will be referred to in this book, is the way in which online course content is organized to manage the learning environment. Learning management is a direct result of effective course organization. If the course content is properly organized based on the online instructor's course goals and teaching style, the students will have the best opportunity to master major course objectives.

Traditional face-to-face classroom instructors have a distinct advantage over online instructors when considering course organization. Students in the traditional classroom have an understanding of the teaching methods employed by the majority of instructors. Instructors may lecture, organize students into groups, or implement a project-based curriculum. These course organizational structures are familiar to most students, and therefore students will assimilate without experiencing any of the cognitive dissonance often associated with a new or unknown teaching style.

Online instructors face the challenge of presenting their course content in a meaningful way in the online setting. This is a complex challenge: The course should be organized in an intuitive way that students can easily navigate, and content should be presented in a way that leads to high levels of student learning. Overcoming these challenges requires careful planning and deliberate development of course navigation and organization. Online instructors can work within their learning management system to develop a course organization that fits their teaching style, content, and student population.

Course Navigation

All popular online learning management systems generate course templates with a ready-to-use course menu. For example, the Blackboard LMS uses a default menu, as shown in table 3.1.

The navigation menu should be organized and named more intuitively than the provided default template. It is unclear using the default navigation where students will find their assignments, quizzes, or tests. "Content" may be used for course materials and "Information" for course information and resources, but these terms are too ambiguous for many students to immediately discern. For this reason, it is important for online instructors to be more thoughtful when choosing how to name the navigation menu items.

Many instructors react to the default navigation menu by adding multiple new menu items with more specific names. This is a good practice as long as the instructor deletes the other items. Leaving unused items in the course menu will only result in confusion for the students. A good practice is to attempt to build the menu with as few items as possible. However, this practice should be balanced with the thought that students should never be more than a few mouse clicks away from an assignment or content area.

Table 3.1. Blackboard LMS Default Menu Items

Home Page	The page that students see when they log into the course
Content	A content page where instructors can include course content
Information	A content page where instructors can include course information
Discussions	A page with discussion board forums for student interaction
Tools	A list of tools available to instructors and students in Blackboard

Variety of Learning Activities

Another consideration of course organization and learning management should be a variety of learning activities. Students' learning needs are as diverse as their personalities; therefore, it is important that online instructors give all students an opportunity to show their mastery of the content in a variety of ways. Some students are more comfortable completing traditional multiple-choice and short-answer tests and quizzes, while others prefer assignments with deliverables like a paper or presentation and still others prefer to work in a group setting with their classmates.

Learning activity variety should also be balanced with the idea that the activity types within the course should be repeated throughout the semester. Variety is important, but it should not be the only consideration when developing new assignments. Students who are allowed to familiarize themselves with an assignment type will produce better results with each submission opportunity; therefore, online instructors should identify three to five assignment types that assess the course content in a meaningful way and use them on a regular basis.

Higher-Order and Critical Thinking Opportunities

A valid criticism of the current state of online learning in higher education is that instructors often rely too heavily on assignments that can be graded automatically by the LMS. Multiple-choice, matching, and true-or-false quizzes and tests fall into this category. Instructors who choose to use only these types of assessment activities within their online courses are depriving their students of the opportunity to develop a deeper understanding of the course content.

Implementing assignments that cause students to think critically about true-to-life situations and then apply their newly acquired knowledge to those situations illustrate the students' level of content mastery. These opportunities are important for both instructors and students: Instructors can use this type of assessment to gain a better understanding of student perception and understanding, while students are forced to grapple with the content, resulting in academic growth.

TOOLS FOR COURSE ORGANIZATION AND LEARNING MANAGEMENT

Content Pages

Within any of the popular learning management systems, instructors can create content areas or content pages to group course content appropriately according to their teaching style. Items on the course navigation menu are often associated with content pages that contain the content suggested by the item name. A menu item called "Learning Modules" takes students to a content page with each learning module for the course; similarly, a menu item named "Home Page" navigates back to the content page where students start when they log in to the course.

Content pages can also be linked to other parts of the course using a variety of methods that differ slightly with each LMS. For the purpose of learning management, instructors use content pages to group learning activities and resources that will contribute to students' understanding of a specific course topic or learning objective. It is also common practice to group the assessment for the course objective on the same content page as learning activities and resources.

Learning Modules

Where learning activities and assignments grouped together by content and chronology are called *units* in the traditional classroom, many online courses refer to the same grouping of activities as *learning modules*. A learning module is created when an instructor groups together course activities, resources, and assignments that address a common set of objectives. Learning modules are generally developed to be completed in chronological order, and therefore activities within each module are displayed in the order that students should access them.

Like traditional learning units, learning modules are grouped based on natural breaks in the curriculum. Some instructors choose to create multiple modules by breaking the curriculum into manageable pieces using date ranges, such as weekly, bimonthly, or monthly modules; other instructors break the curriculum into manageable pieces that culminate with major course assessments such as tests, projects, or presentations. Whichever method an instructor chooses, the modules should be listed in the order in which students should complete them.

Learning Module Planning

Just as the overall structure and organization of the course should be well thought out and strategically planned, so should the structure of each learning module. Typically, once the instructor has decided which learning objectives will be addressed in each learning module, he or she will begin planning how to teach and to assess each objective within the module.

A good planning technique is to storyboard each module by creating a flowchart that starts with an objective and flows to the learning activity and then to the assessment. This can be done for each objective in the module. Once the storyboard is finished, the instructor can then begin to annotate the flowchart, adding which technology tools and media will be used to develop the learning activity and which assessment type will best assess the students' mastery of the objective. It is also important to understand that many objectives can be evaluated using the same module assessment.

Assessment Activities for the Online Environment

Assessment in the online course environment can be conducted using a variety of engaging activities. Assessment activities can range from strategies that are similar to those used in the traditional face-to-face classroom to those that could not be conducted without the use of the technology associated with an online course. Papers, quizzes, and tests can be assigned and graded much like they are administered in a traditional classroom, while discussions, presentations, and group projects must be structured quite differently.

We will discuss assessment in the online course environment in detail in a later chapter; however, the following section will introduce various assessment activities that are frequently used to manage learning in an online course. This section will also discuss some appropriate strategies to implement each activity, as well as how students should prepare and submit their deliverables.

Quizzes and Tests

Quizzes and tests constructed of multiple-choice, short-answer, matching, and true-or-false questions can be built and administered using the LMS's built-in tools. Instructors can use LMS tools to add a variety of question types to quizzes or tests, which can be set to be automatically graded by the system. Automatically graded quizzes and tests give students the opportunity to receive instant feedback after submitting.

Automatically graded tests and quizzes are also useful for keeping the online instructor's workload more manageable. Many online instructors use automatically graded tests and quizzes to assess their students' reading of the assigned material, to check students' understanding mid-module, or to administer large exams such as midterms and finals.

Test and quizzes can be set up to draw questions randomly from a large pool, and to allow students multiple attempts to master the material. These strategies work well together because students will not take the exact same assessment each time, but each will cover the same objectives.

Papers

Assignments that require students to submit a paper of any length—whether it be research, a book report, creative writing, or other written work—can be created within the LMS as well. The submission item allows students to upload digital files just as they would add an attachment to an e-mail. Instructors can then access the item and grade it according to the assignment requirements.

When creating the item where students will submit their paper, it is good practice to attach any directions, rubrics, links, and other resources that students will need to complete the assignment. Grouping the assignment directions and resources with the submission item will prevent students from becoming confused about where to turn in their assignment.

A distinct advantage of having students submit papers through an online LMS is protection against plagiarism. Many learning management systems can be integrated with software that checks student work against academic and popular sources upon submission. If the LMS or institution does not offer plagiarism checking at submission, instructors can still submit the digital files to plagiarism-detection websites. Checking for plagiarism using these services is impossible without a digital file, so even traditional face-to-face instructors may choose to use an LMS to collect student work of this type.

Student Presentations

Presentation projects are popular assessment activities in many traditional face-to-face courses and can also be used as a valuable assessment tool in online courses. Submission of the presentation for credit can be set up in the same way as that for paper submissions because this submission type allows students to upload any digital media or file. Because most online courses are conducted asynchronously, students will not have the opportunity to present live in front of their classmates and instructor; however, this should not prevent instructors from using this tool.

The most basic way for students to complete presentation assignments in an online course is to create presentations using a slide presentation tool. Students can add speaking notes to each slide to help the instructor understand how they would present their ideas given the opportunity. Perhaps a better method is to have the students create a screen recording of their presentation using popular free screen-recording software such as the Google Chrome plug-in Screencastify, Screencast-O-Matic, or Bandicam. Students can record voiceovers while moving through their presentations in much the same way that they would in a live classroom.

Discussions

All popular learning management systems have a discussion board, a tool designed to help online instructors mimic the valuable conversation that happens in a traditional face-to-face classroom. Like the presentations, discussion can be facilitated online, but it will be different in many ways. Within the discussion board, instructors can create individual forums that focus the discussion on particular topics.

One major difference between online discussion boards and face-to-face discussion in a traditional classroom is that online discussion happens asynchronously, so when students reply to the discussion prompt, they may not receive comments from other students for a few hours, or even a few days. It is up to the instructor to structure discussion assignments in a way that promotes active and frequent participation. This can be done by requiring a set number of responses by certain dates, developing engaging and sometimes polarizing discussion topics, and being active as the instructor on the discussion board.

Blogs

The term *blog* was created by truncating the term *Weblog*. A blog is an informal, public online journal of one's thoughts, ideas, and reflections. Online instructors can use blogs to allow students to share their thoughts and reflections on important course materials such as textbook chapters, primary source documents, or videos. Most popular learning management systems include a blog tool; however, there are also many free blogging platforms available on the web.

The strength of a blog is that students can share their responses to higher-order questions about the course content with their classmates and their instructor. It is often helpful for other students to see how their peers reacted to the exact same material that they read, watched, or listened to. As with discussion boards, it is productive to require students to respond to a number of their peers' blog posts to engage in discourse that further scaffolds the learning. Using blogs on a regular basis allows an instructor the opportunity to see how their students' understanding of the course content has developed over the semester.

TECHNIQUES FOR COURSE ORGANIZATION
AND LEARNING MANAGEMENT

Modular Course Organization

Learning modules were discussed in some detail earlier in this chapter. In all online course organizational structures, some variation of a learning module will be used. However, a course that is built using a modular course organization structure will revolve around the learning module content area. The learning module content area should be clearly labeled as a menu item, and the instructor should encourage students to visit that area each time they log in to the course.

Learning modules built within the learning module content area should be organized chronologically, as described earlier in this chapter, and labeled clearly. Since learning modules are set up in chronological order and should be accessed in sequential order instructors can provide suggested pacing to the students by labeling the modules with start and end dates. Date ranges in the module labels or descriptions help students to navigate directly to the module in which they should be working when they log in to the course. The students merely need to check the date and look for the module that includes that date within its date range.

Each learning module should include a variety of learning activities and assessments that apply to a set of related learning objectives. Learning modules should begin with a short introductory item that describes which objectives will be covered and which activities students should expect to see within the module. Many instructors find it helpful to also include a suggested pacing guide within the module to help students meet the appropriate deadlines for major deliverables.

Culminating Summative Assessment-Based Modular Organization

An effective way to structure the learning modules in an online course is to develop each module with common objectives that will be assessed with a cumulative exam. The use of cumulative exams to finalize units of the curriculum is a common practice in teaching and learning. Students are accustomed to this process, and therefore they can more quickly understand online learning modules that are structured in this way.

Learning modules developed around a cumulative assessment are often built by creating several smaller assignments and activities that are associated with a portion of the objectives. Once all objectives have been thoroughly taught and assessed individually, students then prove their knowledge on the cumulative exam. Structuring the learning modules around a few cumulative exams helps students to better understand how each grouping of objectives fits together overall.

Case-Based Modular Organization

Earlier in this chapter, discussion board forums and blogs were discussed as methods of assessing students' understanding of complex topics covered in readings and other course materials. These tools provide great methods to implement case-based learning opportunities for students. Many courses have curricula that can be effectively assessed by requiring students to analyze case studies and discuss them with their peers and the instructor. Case studies can be powerful tools for courses that explore ethics or real-world applications, or those that have a management focus.

To effectively implement case-based modular organization, instructors should break their curriculum into aligned objectives that can be effectively expressed and assessed by content-related case studies. Each module should be built around the case in question, with the students performing small assessments that address individual components of the content and the case itself as the culminating assessment for the module. Students should be required to analyze the case specifically based on the module objectives. An effective method for student discussion of the case studies in detail is to organize the students into cohort groups for the duration of the class.

Cohort Groups

Many traditional classroom instructors choose to assign several group projects to assess students throughout the duration of the course. This is often a point of contention with online instructors because they do not feel confident that group projects can be effectively implemented in the online environment. However, most learning management systems have tools that help instructors organize their students into groups and to provide a course link where group members can collaborate. As group members become more familiar with one another, they are able to communicate and collaborate more effectively with one another.

Once organized into cohort groups of four to eight students, those students will participate in many course assignments with only their cohort members. This setup works well for group projects and presentations, just as it would in a traditional face-to-face course. Students must learn ways to communicate effectively with their online classmates, but this can be accomplished using one of the many free videoconferencing technologies available to students.

They can also communicate via e-mail and using LMS-specific chat rooms or discussion forums.

Organizing students into smaller groups for discussion board forums places additional responsibility on each student to participate because individuals cannot hide as easily as they could in a whole-class discussion. Students in cohort groups also tend to perform better on group projects than those in classes where cohorts are not established, because they already have familiarity with their group members, each other's schedules, and preferred methods of communication.

TIPS FOR COURSE ORGANIZATION AND LEARNING MANAGEMENT

- Create navigation for your online course that is intuitive for students to follow. Students should be able to find everything in the class after spending just a few minutes familiarizing themselves with the course navigation.

- Name your course navigation buttons carefully according to where they lead. The navigation buttons should have names that explicitly refer to what the students will need to do in that area of the course.

- Avoid navigation menu names like "Information" or "Content"; instead, use names like "Learning Modules" and "Project Resources."

- Keep the course navigation menu short. Avoid adding more than five buttons to the course navigation menu to avoid overlap and confusion.

- Implement a variety of learning activities and assignments. Students should be taught and assessed in multiple ways to prevent bias.

- Create learning modules by separating the course curriculum into manageable chunks based on similar learning objectives.

- Use a storyboard or flowchart to help plan each module by connecting each objective to a learning activity and an assessment.

- Implement automatically graded quizzes and tests to check students' understanding of reading assignments important to the curriculum.

- Develop quizzes and tests using large question pools and random selection to prevent collusion among students.

- Submit students' papers and presentations to available plagiarism-detection web-based services to ensure academic integrity.

- Assign presentation projects that require students to submit screen recordings of their presentation slides along with voiceover narration.

- Require student participation in discussion board forums by creating a timeline for responses that is associated with their grade.

- Keep discussion boards active by posting responses to students on a regular basis. Students are generally more active when they know the instructor is reading and responding on a regular basis.

- Require students to read and comment on their classmates' blog post assignments. This will expose students to multiple points of view on the same content.

- Use modular course organization when your curriculum has natural breaks in objectives that can be assessed with multiple-choice and short-answer exams.

- Use case-based modular organization when you are teaching courses that lend themselves to analyzing real-world events like history, political science, and ethics.

- Use cohort groups to help students establish connections with the classmates they will be working closely with on projects, presentations, and discussions throughout the course.

Chapter 4

Building Communication and Effective Communication

Closing the Gap between the Online Instructor and Online Students

Dr. Anel Chen sat in her office entering grades to close out the semester. She couldn't help but notice that in her online systems analysis class she had significantly fewer As and Bs and significantly more Cs and Ds than in her face-to-face systems analysis class. Anel concluded that this was because her teaching style relied heavily on building strong relationships and student rapport through classroom discussions.

Anel realized that the same level of collaboration between her and her students, and among the students themselves, was not happening in the online classroom. She could not conceive of how she would be able to better collaborate with her students through a computer screen. Anel needed help before the start of next semester.

COMMUNITY AND COMMUNICATION IN THE ONLINE CLASSROOM

Community can be defined as a sense of fellowship within a group of individuals who share common characteristics and goals. This simple definition is applicable to the online learning environment. Students enrolled in online courses share similar characteristics in that they are all students working together in a learning environment, whether it is a college course, high school class, professional development module, or any of the myriad applications of online instruction.

Online students at every level usually share the goal of successfully completing the course or training module. However, an online learning environment may contain barriers to the creation of fellowship, and this

29

lack of fellowship is often detrimental to successful online learning. This chapter will explore tools, techniques, and tips for successfully building a community of online learners.

TOOLS FOR BUILDING
COMMUNITY AND COMMUNICATION

Calendar

A course calendar is a basic communication tool for online teaching. By communicating deadlines, reminders, and due dates on the calendar, instructors are preparing students for success. It is important to set the calendar dates before the course begins and to make as few modifications as possible. If a modification is made, make sure to communicate that information to students promptly. Referring to the calendar while communicating with students is another way to use this tool.

E-mail

E-mail—another basic communication tool—is a quick and efficient way to communicate with students. However, e-mail does have pitfalls. While it is nice to respond quickly to a student's question, a hastily written e-mail may come across as terse or impersonal. Instructors should take time to respond personally, giving an appropriate salutation containing the student's name, responding to all parts of the question being asked, and soliciting further questions from the student. It takes time to respond in this way, but the care added in responding to e-mails will go a long way in creating an environment of open communication.

It is also important to set guidelines for e-mail correspondence. This includes a reminder that e-mail responses are not immediate and can be expected during regular business hours. These issues will be addressed later in this chapter.

Announcements Page

Announcements are usually incorporated in the home page or opening page of an online course shell, allowing the instructor to call attention to new information and remind students of pending due dates and assignments. Instructors should direct students' attention to the announcements often at the beginning of a course to instill in them the habit of checking for updated information. By checking regularly updated announcements, students will gain a sense of continuous communication with the instructor.

Screencasts

A screencast is a digital recording of a computer screen that usually contains audio narration. This tool allows instructors to present material to students in a format that may be viewed and reviewed at any time. Screencasts promote communication because the instructor is verbally giving information rather than posting presentations for students to review. Hearing the instructor's voice allows students to become more familiar and comfortable with the instructor. There are many inexpensive and free products and websites that may be used to create screencasts.

Video Recordings

Video recordings have long been a part of face-to-face classroom instruction, so it should not be surprising that videos are an important part of the online classroom. Instructors may choose to provide instruction by asking students to view informational videos containing content pertinent to the course. Instructors may also record videos of their classroom lectures. Video recordings provide course content that may be viewed at any time. This relieves students from the pressure of committing to a specific class time, which enhances the online classroom experience.

While video recordings are useful for conveying content, instructors must remain cognizant of copyright and make sure all laws related to copyright are followed. This includes seeking permissions and using open-source material.

Another useful video-recording tool for online instructors is annotated video. An annotation tool allows the instructor to add text, links, and notations of important information. to a video recording, prompting students to pay specific attention to certain material. Students may also create annotated video recordings of their classroom assignments and presentations. The instructor may then respond to the students' annotations, providing the two-way communication that is sometimes lost in the online environment. There are free and inexpensive video annotation tools found on the internet that may enhance online instruction.

Online Chat

Online chat is a communication tool that offers real-time text messages to senders and receivers in an online environment. Chat sessions may take place with an entire classroom of students discussing a topic with the instructor and usually centers around some type of slide presentation or previous reading assignment.

Chat sessions may also occur in small groups determined by the instructor. Student chat sessions may be recorded and reviewed by the instructor. This allows the instructor to monitor the content of the discussions and provide pertinent feedback to students related to the content and questions arising in the student chat sessions.

Discussion Boards

Another online communication tool is a discussion board. A discussion board is an online discussion site where students may hold conversations by posting messages to the class. There are many options for curating a discussion board. Instructors may choose to post a discussion question for their students and set a time limit for responses.

Discussion responses may address the posted question or may break off into threads responding to other questions that come up as the discussion evolves. The instructor may choose to participate in the ongoing discussion or create a synopsis at the close of the discussion and then respond to thoughts and questions from students.

Instructors may also choose to post a question to the discussion board with a short time limit for responses, then assign a student to create a short synopsis of the initial discussion and pose questions of his or her own. This may be done several times throughout the discussion, with several students being assigned to create a synopsis and pose further questions.

In another effective use of a discussion board, the instructor posts a question at the beginning of the discussion and requires students to post a set number of responses to the question and a set number of responses to postings by their classmates. Online discussions are structured conversations that require students to interact with their peers and the instructor on a regular basis. This is an invaluable tool for building an online community.

Regardless of how the discussions are planned, it is important that the instructor has a presence in the discussion. Simply posting a weekly question and counting responses will not build the sense of community that is necessary in online instruction. By actively participating in the discussion, instructors help build relationships with students and get a sense of students' strengths and needs.

Synchronous Discussions

A synchronous discussion is an online discussion that takes place in real time. These may be simple audio discussions or may also contain a video of the participants. The advantage to synchronous online discussions is that both instructor and students get a better sense of tone and body language. While discussion through chat and discussion boards may be effective in conveying information, it does not provide the communication cues that are present in a synchronous online discussion.

These synchronous discussions may be recorded for students to review or as a way for absent students to access important course material. Synchronous online discussions may take place within the course shell or may occur by way of tools such as Skype and Google Hangouts, which may be easier to access for students lacking a strong internet connection.

Social Media

Social media are computer-mediated technologies that promote the creation and sharing of information and ideas within virtual communities. These virtual communities are a good fit for supporting the online teaching environment. Participating in these online environments can also lead to the development of professional learning communities.

A *professional learning community* (PLC) is a group of people who share common academic goals and attitudes and meet semi-regularly to collaborate on classwork. A PLC can be created by students within class or by students pursuing a particular field of study or interest area. Online instructors may also use social media tools such as Twitter, blogs, and wikis to create a PLC within a course.

Twitter is a social networking platform that allows members to microblog or create short posts known as *tweets*. Instructors may tweet information, web links, videos, assignments, and so on to students enrolled in a course and require responses from those students. Twitter may also be used as an online chat tool if a class tweet session is scheduled for a certain time.

As discussed in chapter 3, blogs are regularly updated websites written in an informal, conversational style. Blogs may be used by online instructors to communicate class updates and news or to host class discussions. The instructor might create a blog post containing course information followed by a question. Students would then be expected to participate in a class conversation by responding to the post. Students might also be required to research a topic and create the initial post and pose a question for discussion.

A wiki is a website that allows collaborative editing of the content of the site by member users. Course information may be contained within the wiki, and class members may be invited to interact with that information. This might take the form of researching and adding relevant information, participating in an embedded blog or discussion board, working in small groups to create class presentations, or any other collaboration created by the instructor.

Telephone

Perhaps one of the simplest tools for communication with online students is the telephone. Instructors may call individual students at regular intervals during the course period to check in on the student's progress, questions, or triumphs. These calls should be scheduled either individually or during a block of time scheduled in the course calendar. Students also need to feel free to call the instructor's office or professional telephone number with concerns. This might be during office hours or during a set block of time scheduled in the course calendar.

Cell phones also support many of the tools discussed in this chapter. Applications for cell phones provide instant access to course materials and collaborations. With a cell phone, students may e-mail, access websites and social media, chat, and participate in live video discussions.

TECHNIQUES FOR BUILDING
COMMUNITY AND COMMUNICATION

Discussion Board Techniques

A discussion board can be a powerful tool for online teaching. There are many techniques for integrating the discussion board into instruction. An introduction discussion board is a practical technique for introducing the discussion board and building community. On an introduction discussion board, students are asked to introduce themselves and share some information about their lives. Classmates post introductions and then make connections with other students by responding to a set number of introductions. This simple discussion board activity sets a foundation for building community throughout the semester.

Another popular technique is to post a question for discussion with a set response time. This usually involves a required number of posts to the discussion board and includes responses to a minimum number of posts by classmates. While this method can lead to a robust discussion, it is best suited to small group discussions. Used with an entire class, this technique may lead to the first responses being well thought out and well written, while the later responses become word-dense repetitions of the first posts. In other words, it becomes a race to see which student gets to answer the question well and which students are forced to reiterate the first posts.

One technique that alleviates the issue of duplication is to post a question for a few days, do a summary of the initial posts, and then pose another question for a few days and summarize again. This can be done several times throughout the discussion period. In order to build ownership of the discussion and community within the class, students may be assigned to create the intra-discussion summaries and questions to be posted.

A single discussion board does not have to be used with the entire class. Several discussion boards may be set up within a class so that small groups of students may participate at the same time with the same questions without competing for the best responses. The use of small groups also helps build a sense of community because students in a small group tend to communicate outside of class and build relationships within the group.

Another small group technique asks students to research a specific topic. This could include websites, articles, primary source documents, or any other artifacts relevant to the topic. Students in each group work together to create a resource document that is then posted to the class discussion board. After the documents have been reviewed by all students, a discussion question related to the topic is posted for the whole class to discuss.

The technique of hosting a debate is also used by many instructors. To host a debate, small groups are assigned two sides of a topic and given time to research and create their position. The topics are then posted one at a time and the two small groups assigned to the given topic make the case for their position. Classmates outside the two small groups pose questions and responses to the positions presented. This process is repeated until all groups' positions have been presented. The class then votes on which groups best presented their arguments.

A final discussion board technique is to ask an expert in the field to act as a guest host for the discussion board. The expert introduces him- or herself to the class and opens the board for questions. Students post a minimum number of questions and responses to the expert, which creates a strong discussion. The expert then ends the discussion by creating a brief summary or highlight post.

Synchronous Discussion Techniques

Synchronous discussions need a focus to be successful. Some instructors assign questions to help guide the discussions, while others actively participate in discussions and present information through either lectures or slide presentations.

One technique for guiding questions is to assign small group discussion and assign each group member a role to perform. The discussion roles vary depending on the content of the course, but sample roles include someone to lead the discussion, someone to question the text, someone to present the new vocabulary, and someone to direct attention to important passages in the text. Another way to use guided questions is to provide a list of questions and ask students to prepare responses to the questions. When the discussion begins, a lead discussant poses the questions in order and then allows time for students to share their responses.

When presenting a slide presentation in a synchronous discussion, it is important to remember that the slides should contain only the highlights of the information presented and the instructor should verbally provide details to support the highlights. It is also important to remember that the slides should lead to discussion, and the instructor should pause to allow this. Embedding questions into the slide presentation can also help focus the discussion.

Instructor Presence Techniques

Students need to "see" the instructor as part of the day-to-day workings of the course. This creates a sense of the community and breaks down barriers between student and instructor. Instructors should make presence a priority for their online instruction. That means instructors should regularly post announcements, create discussion board posts, and interact with students to develop a class presence.

In order to build a presence in the online classroom, the instructor must work to demonstrate interaction with the course. It is important to remember that online courses are meant to function much the same as a traditional classroom, with ongoing teacher and student interaction rather than independent study of a given topic.

Creating a sense of presence may begin on the first day of the course with an instructor introduction. Instructors may introduce themselves in many ways. Posting photographs or introductory videos allows students to visualize the instructor and provides a personal touch. Some instructors choose to create a narrative that tells about their lives and careers, while others host live video sessions that also allow for student questions.

Providing continuous and consistent feedback is another technique for creating presence. Some instructors are able to post to discussion boards and grade assignments on a daily basis, while others choose to set a specific day or days each week for those activities. There is no right or wrong time to provide feedback, but communicating when it is to happen and sticking to that schedule is important in developing your class presence because students may take comfort in consistent feedback and not develop feelings of estrangement with the instructor.

Seeking student feedback is another technique for developing presence. Many instructors regularly ask students for feedback about how they are doing. This can be done by e-mailing all students with a few questions related to the instructor's presence, or done by individually e-mailing each student and asking for open-ended feedback. While individual e-mails are time consuming, the reward can be worth the effort. Individual e-mails to students provide a direct avenue for communication that enhances classroom presence.

Another technique for developing presence involves appropriate use of nonverbal cues. Online students communicate primarily through written text, with no body language aid in interpreting it. When communicating with students, instructors should remember to follow standard grammar rules, include salutations, and avoid quick, terse replies. Taking time to address the student by name, fully answer all parts of the student's question, and indicate a willingness to follow up if there is still confusion will improve communication with students.

TIPS FOR BUILDING
COMMUNITY AND COMMUNICATION

- *Set parameters.* The online classroom is not open 24 hours a day, seven days a week. Let students know when to expect communication to occur.

- *Maintain high expectations.* Communicating to students that you expect them to complete assignments, participate in discussions, and communicate with you is an important step in helping students achieve success.

- *Post pictures.* Having students post pictures of themselves allows everyone to visualize the people they are communicating with online.

- *Set due dates.* Setting due dates at the beginning of the semester and communicating those deadlines allows students to create a plan for completing assignments.

- *Provide rubrics.* Giving specific expectations for assignments allows students to set their goals for success.

- *Remind students of due dates.* Frequently reminding students of due dates communicates the importance of completing work on time.

- *Be patient.* Sometimes technological tools don't work. Communicating that this is understood may relieve student stress.

- *Embed a librarian.* Making a direct connection with the library provides another person for students to go to when they lack information.

- *Participate.* Frequent participation in discussion boards and other interactions will develop a stronger presence in the online classroom.

- *Provide examples.* Although written descriptions for assignments may be thorough, examples of exemplary work provide a model of instructor expectations.

- *Provide structure.* It's important for students to know exactly what is expected in discussion posts, discussion responses, and written assignments.

- *Intervene when necessary.* If one student is dominating class discussions, reach out to him or her privately and provide some guidance.

- *Redirect the discussion.* At times, discussions may veer off track. Don't hesitate to redirect the discussion.

- *Encourage communication.* Frequently ask students to reach out to you if they are confused about any aspect of the online course.

- *Use small groups.* Dividing the class into small groups allows for better peer communication to be established.

- *Provide materials.* Post the course syllabus, class policies, expectations, objectives, and course materials at the beginning of the semester.

- *Require proper netiquette.* Encourage students to ignore misspellings and mechanics during fast-paced discussion. Also, discourage the use of ALL CAPITAL LETTERS, which indicates shouting.

- *Promote duplication.* Encourage students to e-mail themselves a copy of any materials shared with classmates and online submissions. This time-stamps the material in the event of a technological glitch.

- *Demand confidentiality.* Remind students that personal information such as telephone numbers and private e-mail addresses are to be used only for class purposes and are not to be shared without permission.

- *Communicate early.* Make contact with students before the course begins to greet the students and communicate the opening date of the course, required textbooks, and other important information.

Chapter 5

Course Information and Learner Support

Providing Students with Appropriate Learning Support Resources

Dr. Mary Ferguson had just settled down for the evening. She curled up on her sofa with a glass of wine and a good book she had been planning to start for days. She was finally ready for some "me" time. She heard her cell phone ding quietly from the coffee table where she'd left it. The ding signaled that a new e-mail had arrived. Mary decided to ignore the ding and continue to enjoy her evening. But after the tenth ding, the e-mail could not be ignored.

Mary reached for her phone and pressed the e-mail icon. She scrolled through the e-mails listed there. All were from students enrolled in her online course. She sighed quietly to herself. Not only was this barrage of e-mails disrupting her quiet evening, but all of the questions had answers that could easily be found by reading the course syllabus. Mary placed her wine glass and book on the coffee table and began to respond to each e-mail. As she responded, she thought that there must be a way to make sure students understand how to find the answers to questions like these.

COURSE INFORMATION AND LEARNER SUPPORT

The Open SUNY Course Quality Rubric (OSCQR) describes *online course information* as course-specific resource materials for student use.[1] Similarly, the Blackboard Exemplary Course Plan Rubric describes *learner support* as addressing the support resources made available to students taking the course.[2] For the purposes of this book, we will use both terms to refer to any and all materials made available to students by the online instructor.

When students begin an online course, they are often faced with the task of becoming accustomed to the way the course content, assignments, and assessments are presented. Students in a traditional face-to-face classroom have the advantage of immediate access to their instructor for protocol questions and support. Unfortunately, this advantage is not available to students in a fully online course. For this reason, the online instructor needs to provide a rich repository of course-specific resources prior to the beginning of the course.

With immediate access to a repository of course-specific resources, students are able to access the answers to their technical and protocol questions without waiting for an instructor response. An effective online instructor will strive to support students by providing information, such as:

- where important course readings, lecture presentations, and materials are found
- how to submit course assignments, assessments, and projects
- where due dates and test dates can be found
- syllabus and other important course documents
- course-specific and institution-specific policies
- course-specific technology requirements
- access to accommodations for students with disabilities

The Fixed Cost of Providing
Course Information and Learner Support

Information and support provides an invaluable resource for students, but this task has many added benefits for instructors as well. Online instructors, both new and experienced, often field a large number of questions at the beginning of each new semester. Implementing an approach that provides students with course information and support resources should reduce the overall volume of questions that are frequently asked by students at the beginning of each new course.

The initial workload of creating a repository of course information and student support resources is often large. Many instructors believe that this information could all be included in the course syllabus; however, there are many more aspects to a successful online course that are not traditionally addressed in syllabus design. The endeavor involves curating and creating items that address each question that students frequently ask, as well as any information that the instructor deems most important to student success.

One of the many benefits of teaching an online course is that all popular learning management systems include a function to copy a previous semester's course into future semester course shells. For the online instructor, this functionality ensures that the creation of course information and learner support resources is a one-time endeavor. In financial terms, this scenario is referred to as a *fixed cost*. In other words, once the resources have been created, the instructor does not have to re-create them each semester but continues to benefit from their existence for the foreseeable future. However, it is important with each new semester that the instructor reevaluate and adjust the resources as needed.

Just-in-Time Learner Support

Another aspect of course-specific information and learner support is addressing student concerns and questions that fall outside of the information resources provided as well as those that are covered in the provided resources but are still asked by students. When an instructor immediately responds to communication from a student using electronic means to address a question or concern, it is referred to as just-in-time (JIT) feedback.

Instructors should consider the content and timing of their responses when addressing incoming student concerns. Student questions and concerns with answers that are not found in the provided course information and learner support resources should be handled with a direct answer in a timely manner. However, student questions and concerns that can be found in the provided course information and learner support resources could be met with one of the following responses:

- Please refer to the provided resources to find an answer to your question.
- Please refer to the syllabus under the appropriate section to find an answer to your question.
- Please review all of the provided course information and support resources before communicating any questions or concerns to your instructor.

Responding in the above manner often addresses an issue that has come to be known as *baby bird syndrome*. Baby birds in the nest expect their mother to attend to their every need without attempting to find a solution for themselves. In the same way, students can develop a tendency to inquire of the instructor as soon as they encounter an issue without first searching for the answer in the provided information and resources. Effective instructors cater their responses to student questions by encouraging them to find answers for themselves instead of simply feeding it to them whenever they squawk.

TOOLS FOR INFORMATION AND SUPPORT

Welcome Announcement and E-mail

The first tool in the online instructor's toolbox is an introductory e-mail or announcement using the LMS's announcement feature. Many learning management systems have an announcement feature that can be set to send an e-mail message in addition to posting the announcement. This feature is beneficial because the information can be found by students in two places: within the course and in their e-mail.

The structure of the introductory announcement is the first step in helping the student become oriented to the course. The announcement should begin with a general welcome message that begins the semester-long process of building student rapport. It is important for instructors to use the first few lines to make the students understand that their instructor cares about their academic and personal growth.

The next portion of the introductory message should outline some specifics about the course itself. This could be information about how to navigate the course as well as where students can find the repository of course information and learner support resources. Students will appreciate some direction when they log into the course for the first time. This will alleviate significant stress for many students at the beginning of the semester.

Finally, the introductory message should contain a call to action for students. The call to action can be any number of activities. The instructor may wish to invite the students to find and print the course syllabus, review the technical information, or post in an introductory discussion forum. Any activity that requires students to navigate the course and perform an action will begin their orientation to the course.

Example Introductory Message

Hello All,

My name is Professor Smith, and I am very excited to be your instructor for Introduction to American History. I have no doubt that we will have a successful semester! This course will be fully online, which means that there will be no face-to-face requirements. All of your assignments, tests, quizzes and projects will be submitted through the learning management system.

When you log into the course, the first item on the course menu is called "Start Here." This is where you will find all of the course documents, such as the syllabus, schedule, and major assignment descriptions.

After you have taken some time to explore the course, please print the syllabus and complete the syllabus quiz found on the "Start Here" page. The syllabus quiz is worth 10 points and can be taken up to three times to ensure you have thoroughly examined this important document.

I hope that you all find this course to be an engaging experience!

Sincerely,
Professor Smith

Introduction and Overview Items

Creating short introduction and overview items throughout the online course is an effective way to support learners with the information they need at the time that they need it. Two- or three-sentence descriptions to begin each online course page and learning module will provide students with the needed context to begin. Students will become accustomed to using the introduction items to help guide them through parts of the course that they are seeing for the first time.

A good approach is to develop a short introduction item for each unique part of the course. This could include an introduction describing the course resource page (like the one mentioned earlier in the chapter, entitled "Start Here"), a description of the course content pages, and a thorough description of the assignment types included with each new assignment.

Introductory items for the course pages should include details about what students will find on the page and what they are expected to do while on the page. Introductory items for the course modules should include the major learning objectives for the educational sequence and a description of what students will be expected to accomplish while completing the assigned activities and assessments.

Introductory items that describe assignment types will help students to better meet the expectations for each. Each description should indicate to the students where the resources they will need to complete the assignment are located, as well as where they will find any specific grading requirements or rubrics. Finally, the description should include the due dates and any late work policy pertaining to the assignment.

Example Introductory Item for a Course Orientation Module

Welcome to the Course Orientation Module. In this module you will find many valuable course policies and resources. Look for the following items on this page:

- *Course Introduction Screencast: This video walkthrough will help you to orient yourself to the structure of this course.*
- *Course Syllabus: This is your blueprint for success in this course.*
- *Course Schedule: This document contains all major due dates for assignments and activities.*
- *Syllabus Quiz: This 10-point assignment will assess your understanding of the important information in the syllabus. Please complete it by the due date.*

Syllabus

One of the most important documents of any course—whether fully online or traditional face-to-face—is the course syllabus. The syllabus functions as a blueprint for students to follow throughout the course. A well-constructed syllabus includes a description of the major course deliverables and their due dates, test and quiz due dates, and major objectives to be addressed throughout the course assignments and activities.

Effective online instructors can leverage the power of the syllabus by including information specific to the online course offering. It is helpful to include information that describes the structure of the online course, such as whether it will require any synchronous online sessions or face-to-face sessions, or if it will be fully asynchronous. The syllabus is one of the first opportunities an instructor has to provide students with specific course information and learner support.

Syllabus Quiz

A common problem experienced by instructors is a perceived lack of attention paid by students to the information found in the syllabus. This problem is enhanced for online courses because a comprehensive understanding of the information and policies found in the syllabus is more significant to online students. The solution to this problem is to assess the students' understanding of the syllabus. The assessment of students understanding is commonly referred to as a *syllabus quiz*.

The syllabus quiz should be built based on the parts of the syllabus that the instructor deems the most important. The best practice is to create ten to fifteen-questions quiz consisting of multiple-choice, matching, or short-answer questions. The syllabus quiz is also most effective when it is low stakes and high opportunity; in other words, the quiz should not be worth as much as the quizzes that assess learning objectives, and as such, students should have multiple opportunities to achieve mastery of the content.

Once a student has completed the syllabus quiz with a high degree of accuracy, the instructor can feel confident that particular student has read and understands the most important aspects of the course syllabus. For this reason, when constructing the syllabus quiz, instructors should consider the most frequently asked questions at the beginning of previous semesters.

Examples of Syllabus Quiz Questions

- *What is Professor Smith's preferred method of communication?*
- *Where will I find the submission links for all assignments?*
- *What percentage of the overall grade is the midterm exam worth?*
- *What is the first assignment, and when is it due?*

Screencast Course Walkthrough

An effective tool for helping students become oriented to the navigation and overall structure of the course is to implement a screencast course walkthrough. The course walkthrough can be recorded using screencast software; software such as the Google Chrome plug-in Screencastify, Screencast-O-Matic, or Bandicam are appropriate tools that are either completely free or have a limited free version. It is important to have a working microphone available while recording the walkthrough.

After choosing the appropriate software, the instructor utilizes it in conjunction with the microphone to record both the computer screen and the voiceover while taking the students on a tour of the course. It is best if the instructor speaks clearly and with good volume while explaining the main features of the course. It helps to develop a script or storyboard to guide the creation of the walkthrough.

The course walkthrough should begin with a short introduction to the course and a brief description of the course home page. The walkthrough should continue with the instructor selecting each menu item to open the page, then giving a brief description of each. The availability of a course walkthrough greatly reduces the learning curve for students as they first enter the course. The recording will also give the instructor a resource to direct students to if they have questions about where to find a particular assignment, activity, or resource.

Discussion Board Forum

Another important tool for providing course information and learner support is the discussion board feature available in all popular learning management systems. Specifically, the instructor can create a discussion board forum that serves as a repository of popular student questions and answers. In this forum, students are prompted to leave their questions as a reply to the initial post; the instructor can then go through once or twice each week and respond to the questions.

The strength of using the discussion board for this purpose is that it can be accessed by all students at any time. If one student e-mails the instructor with a question and the instructor responds to that student, only one student's question has been answered. It is generally accepted that if one student asks a question then many more have the same question, so answering the question on the discussion board provides the answer to the entire student population.

Example Course Question Discussion Board Prompt

Students,

Please refer to this discussion board forum to address many of the common questions students have when taking this course. It is appropriate to use this forum to ask questions about course navigation, course resources, and assignment submissions. I will respond to the questions posted here on a regular basis. It is not appropriate to use this discussion board forum to ask content-related questions. That will take place in content specific discussion forums, or on a one-on-one basis.

Virtual Office Hours

Virtual office hours are similar to traditional office hours found in the university setting. Whereas traditional office hours are set periods of time during which the instructor is physically in the office and available to address student questions and concerns, virtual office hours are set periods of time during which the instructor is available virtually for student questions and concerns.

Virtual office hours can be conducted in a variety of ways. Instructors may choose to use video chat tools such as Google Hangouts, Skype, or Zoom Meeting. They may also choose to use built-in virtual classroom tools available in their LMS, such as Blackboard Collaborate. These tools allow students to log in to a virtual classroom and address questions and concerns with their instructors in a synchronous way.

It is good practice for instructors to make themselves available to students in this way for five or ten hours each week at various times. Holding virtual office hours in the morning, afternoon, and possibly evening on different days of the week gives students many options to seek support from the instructor at the most convenient time.

TECHNIQUES FOR INFORMATION AND SUPPORT

Course Home Page

All popular learning management systems allow instructors the autonomy to assign the entry page for students in the course. The assigned entry page is commonly referred to as the *course home page*. This landing spot is where many instructors choose to employ many of the course information and learner support tools discussed earlier in this chapter. Because students see this page first as they log into the course, it is a great place to include course announcements, instructor contact information, and upcoming assignment information.

Course announcements should be found on the course home page so that students entering the course will be met with the most up-to-date information from the instructor. The announcements area should be used consistently throughout the semester to regularly provide students new course information and learner support resources. Each announcement should follow a similar setup. The following is one such effective setup:

- Begin with a greeting.
- Let students know what they will be covering in the course in the coming week or module.
- Let students know what will be due in the coming week or module.
- End with a call to action.

Another way to support learners through the use of a course home page is by providing instructor contact information on the home page. This helps students to understand that the instructor is available to assist them whenever they are in need. It is good practice to include your e-mail address, office phone number, office location, and virtual office hours. Including a short description of your preferred method of communication will help to ensure that most of the communication you receive from students comes through the most appropriate method.

Finally, including an item on the course home page that students can use to view the assignments that will be due in the near future helps them to stay up to date with their coursework. Many learning management systems have items that can be added that function as a to-do list for students and are updated regularly with upcoming due dates. These items can also be created and updated by instructors on a weekly basis.

Course Orientation Module

A valuable technique for enhancing the student's understanding of the course information and learner support resources is implementing a *course orientation module.* The course orientation module should be located in the same area of the course as the future content-related modules.

The orientation module should be structured in much the same way that the students will see in future modules. This approach serves two purposes: First, the students will learn the valuable material within the module, and second, they will begin to orient to the way that future content modules will be displayed. Many instructors will choose to title the orientation module in a way that helps students understand its purpose. Some common names include:

- Module 0
- Getting Started
- Course Orientation
- Start Here

The course orientation module should consist of many of the tools discussed earlier in this chapter, such as a screen recording of the course walkthrough, the syllabus and schedule, a link to the introductory discussion board, and the syllabus quiz. Including these items in the course orientation module will incentivize the students because the syllabus quiz and introductory discussion require them to read through the items in the module. Setting up the orientation module with multiple assessments that have due dates will mimic the flow and structure of future modules while introducing students to important course information and documents.

Resource Page

A final technique to increase students' access to course information and learner support resources is building a *resource page*. The resource page should be labeled clearly and include the following sections:

- Course-Specific Resources
- Technical Resources
- Institutional Resources

The course-specific resources section or folder should consist of resources that are unique to the course that you are teaching. Common course resources include links to helpful websites relevant to student activities, primary source research articles, open-source e-books, and video tutorials that will be helpful to students but may not necessarily fit well within the context of one of the course modules. Resources that the instructor creates can also be located in this section. Assignment checklists, note-taking templates, and grading rubrics are common instructor-created resources that students may need to access on a regular basis.

Technical resources should also be organized into a section or folder within the resource page. The technical resources should include links and instructions to any software needed to complete the course, as well as contact information for technical support for general technology and the specific learning management system. Throughout the semester, students may encounter any number of technical issues associated with software and the learning management system. As the instructor, you are a content expert, but in those circumstances students need technical experts; this section of the resource page gives them access to those experts.

Finally, it is helpful to include links and information to any institutional resources that are available to the online student. Many institutions provide resources such as a writing center, a tutoring center, and disability resource center for students who need additional help or services. This section will make those available to students from within the course, so they will not have to attempt to find the appropriate assistance on their own.

TIPS FOR PROVIDING COURSE INFORMATION AND LEARNER SUPPORT

- Create a list that consists of all course information and learner support resources that you believe students will need as they complete the course.

- Develop a plan to respond to students' concerns or questions that can be answered within the provided course information and learner support. Remember to avoid the development of baby bird syndrome.

- Begin each semester with a detailed welcome announcement and e-mail. The announcement message should open a line of communication between instructor and student and guide students toward the course information and learner support resources.

- Develop individual introduction and overview items to include throughout the course that describe the content pages, course activities, and assignment types.

- Reevaluate your course syllabus from the perspective of a new student in your online course. Include information within the syllabus that new students will find helpful when attempting to locate activities and deliverables within your course.

- Build a syllabus quiz to assess students' understanding of the crucial information in the syllabus. The quiz should give the students multiple opportunities at mastery so the instructor can feel confident that each student has read the document.

- Record a course walkthrough video using screencast software. The screencast recording should take students on a tour of the different parts of the course and discuss when they will use the resources found therein.

- Develop a discussion board forum for students to post questions and concerns about course navigation, resources, and submissions. Remember to visit the forum a few times each week to answer the newly posted questions.

- Hold virtual office hours where you will be available 5 to 10 hours each week at varying times throughout the day. Virtual office hours can be held using video meeting software, and conversations can be set up for students on a drop-in or appointment basis.

- Create a course-specific home page that students will see when they log into the course. Include course announcements, instructor contact information, and assignments that are due soon.

- Regularly post announcements to the home page that update students on what they should be doing in the course and where to find their next activity or assignment.

- Use the LMS's built-in due date tool, or develop your own due date item and update it on a weekly basis.

- List all course information and learner support resources and separate them into orientation resources, course-specific resources, technical resources, and institutional resources.

- Compile the orientation resources into an orientation module that students will complete to begin the semester.

- Mimic the structure of a content-related module structure within the orientation module. Be sure to include one or two assessment types within the module.

- Compile the course-specific resources, technical resources, and institutional resources into separate folders or sections on a resource page within the course.

NOTES

1. "About OSCQR," OSCQR Open SUNY Course Quality Review Rubric, accessed December 27, 2017, http://oscqr.org/about-oscqr.

2. "Exemplary Course Program," Blackboard, accessed December 27, 2017, https://www.blackboard.com/consulting-training/training-technical-services/exemplary-course-program.html#.

Chapter 6

Visual Design and Accessibility

Designing a Visually Engaging and Accessible Online Course

Dr. Carlos Fisher was looking at the fully online section of his Introduction to Environmental Science course. He was worried because he had just received an e-mail from the Department of Disability Services informing him that a visually impaired student was enrolled in his online class for the fall. Carlos was worried because he did not know if his course was accessible for students with visual disabilities.

The e-mail mentioned that the student would be using a screen reader, but Carlos wondered how it would interpret the many images he had embedded in the course. He also used several primary source documents that he had scanned and uploaded to his course. He wondered if the screen reader could make sense of those. Carlos knew that his course needed some work, but he was not sure where to start.

VISUAL DESIGN AND ACCESSIBILITY

One of the most important aspects of a successful online course is that it should be designed so that learners can easily navigate and progress through a logical sequence and pace of content and information. Unlike with face-to-face teaching, norms are unable to be set, nor can the design of the course be explained through direct instruction and modeling; therefore, this can be achieved through consistency in the layout of the course and delivery of content.

Standardized course design enables students to focus on learning rather than figuring out how to understand each new course item and page, making it easier to transition from one assignment to another.[1] Recent studies on the implementation of universal design course shells have indicated an increase in learner retention and success.[2]

Complicated course design and inconsistent structure tend to contribute directly to learner confusion and an overall poor online learning experience. Therefore, the layout of the course should begin with good organizational structure.[3] One key factor that can augment organization of an online course is consistency. Elements that ensure consistency include the overall color scheme and page design as well as the layout and structure of learning modules, assignments, and rubrics used for assessment.

Learning modules include information that has been gathered together to detail instruction that covers two or three objectives for the learner. Modules are often presented with subsections such as "Reading Assignments," "Learning Tasks," "Quiz Directions," and so on. A learning module represents the instructor's best hope of guiding the learners' eyes as they navigate the course.

In a face-to-face setting, learners are given reading assignments that provide the basic knowledge, and then lectures or other instructor-led activities can be used to further explain the material. As there is no face-to-face instruction in an online course, the visual design of the module can provide a way of setting context for the learners as they engage with the material in their learning activities. Titles and headings that link to learning content, activities, and assessments should detail specifically what the learners will access.

A second foundational element of successful online course design is sequencing. When online course overviews, informational content, learning activities, and interactions are sequenced in the same order in each module, learners are able to consistently access information. Students will learn to anticipate where to find and how to navigate new course materials when accessing the next module. Consistent sequencing from module to module reduces the cognitive load for students throughout the course because they can easily locate important course content when beginning each new module.

Online course layout and design can be further enhanced through redundancy. Redundancy is when the same documents appear in several locations. This repetition helps learners navigate easily to relevant information without having to search extensively. Redundancy is especially useful for the most important course documents. Instructors may choose to send important documents such as the course syllabus via e-mail, post it in the course resources, and include it in the orientation module of the online course.

TOOLS FOR VISUAL DESIGN AND ACCESSIBILITY

There is no set of standards specifically for online learning layout and design, but there are recommendations and best practices that can be followed and tools that can be used to provide certain advantages in online instruction. For example, Quality Matters is a nationally recognized faculty-centered peer review process designed to certify the quality of online and blended courses. The Quality Matters program is centered around a rubric developed by faculty for faculty based on extensive research and instructional design best practices to guide in developing, maintaining, and reviewing online courses.[4]

According to John Sener, the Quality Matters Rubric has become the most widely used set of standards for the design of online and blended courses.[5] The rubric contains eight main standards. The first standard is that the course contains an effective course overview and introduction that set clear expectations of what learners can expect from the course and instructions about how the course works. The second standard is that the learning competencies or outcomes the learner will be able to do upon the completion of the online course are clearly defined and aligned. The third standard includes effective assessment and measurement of the content, while the fourth includes a variety of instructional materials that ensure that learners can successfully achieve the outlined course objectives and competencies. Course activities and learner interaction are identified in the fifth standard, and the sixth standard includes appropriate course technologies to facilitate course learning. The final two standards include effective learner support and course accessibility and usability for all learners.

In addition to design and layout standards, web accessibility also needs to be determined when designing a course. Web accessibility relies on several components that work together. Some of these include:

- *Web content*: any part of a website (for an online course), including text, images, forms, and multimedia, as well as any markup code, scripts, and applications.
- *User agents*: software that learners use to access web content, including desktop graphical browsers, voice browsers, mobile phone browsers, multimedia players, plug-ins, and other assistive technologies.
- *Authoring tools*: software or services that instructors use to produce web content for a course, including code editors, document conversion tools, content management systems, blogs, database scripts, and other tools.

Tools for Design of Delivery

There are many different ways to deliver content in an online classroom. These vary based on the content's purpose and potential student use. It is important to select the most appropriate delivery tool for each situation based on your students' needs. Below we discuss some popular content delivery options available to online instructors.

Word Documents

Word documents offer an almost universal format that is standard on most personal computers for viewing text and visual information in a document. However, Word documents cannot be viewed in most browsers; therefore, they will need to be downloaded by students before they can be used. Word documents are most appropriate for assignment templates because they can be edited. They are least appropriate for course syllabi, course rubrics, and assignment instructions that students should not edit. Word documents are also easily read by screen readers used by visually impaired students.

Portable Document Format

Portable Document Format (PDF) is a file format that captures all the elements of a printed document as an electronic image that users can view, navigate, and print. PDF files are easily viewed in most browsers and can also be downloaded or printed for student use. PDF files are most appropriate for course syllabi, assignment rubrics, and assignment instructions. They are least appropriate for assignment templates because they cannot be easily edited.

PDF files are accessible to students with screen readers in most cases, but instructors should be sure to convert documents to PDF rather than print to PDF, as printing to PDF creates an image with no discernable text for screen readers and therefore should be avoided at all costs in an online classroom. Saving a Word document as a PDF file maintains the characters in the text and is not a hindrance to the visually impaired.

Digital Images

Digital images, whether they are photographs or graphics, offer visuals that most personal technology tools are able to access. Photos can help break up large chunks of text and increase white space, making the information easier to read. Digital images must also follow accessibility requirements and therefore must be assigned alternative text that can be read by a screen reader for visually impaired students. Most popular learning management systems have built-in alternative text features that instructors can use when they upload images.

PowerPoint Presentations

PowerPoint presentations offer a visually appealing method for delivery of content by providing information through a series of slides. This method can also include integrated audio of the instructor narrating the slides using a built-in feature of newer versions of Microsoft Office. Narrated PowerPoint presentations are useful to present lecture content in an online course. Instructors can also use this tool to more thoroughly explain complicated assignments, projects, and presentations. PowerPoint presentations that are narrated are accessible documents because students with disabilities can access the content in a variety of ways.

Cloud-Based Documents

Online cloud-based documents such as the Google suite of file types offer real-time collaboration and document-authoring tools. Multiple users can edit a document at the same time, while seeing each other's changes instantaneously. Cloud-based document tools are appropriate for students participating in group work, as well as for assignments where the instructor may wish to work closely with the student throughout the process. They are especially valuable if the instructor wants to give feedback throughout multiple drafts of a paper or project.

Online Slide-Based Presentation Tools

Online slide-based presentation tools such as Slide Share, Prezi, and Google Slides provide an efficient way to offer material in a visually appealing instructor-led manner and, as added advantage they take up little space on a computer. Because these applications are web-based, they can be accessed from any computer. Online slide tools can also be embedded in the online course site so students can view the content on the course page, eliminating the need to follow a link or download a file.

Online Videos

Open-source video platforms such as YouTube, TED, and TeacherTube offer the delivery of video content through an online platform that is accessible on most technology devices. Online videos can be embedded in the online course, which eliminates the need for students to follow a link to the web page where they are found. Students following a link to a video with important course content may watch the video on the web page and then succumb to the temptation of other videos available there. Providing students with links to videos rather than embedding them in the course is analogous to sending a student outside of the face-to-face classroom to find important course content. It is almost always a better idea to keep the students in the learning environment.

The majority of these tools allow for closed-captioning of the content for hearing-impaired learners, but instructors need to carefully choose videos that have that feature enabled. This is especially important if students will be required to complete a course assignment based on the content of the video. Providing supplementary videos throughout the course is a good strategy to increase student understanding, but the instructor is responsible to ensure that this supplemental material is accessible to all students enrolled in the course.

TECHNIQUES FOR VISUAL DESIGN AND ACCESSIBILITY

Visual Style

Course pages should be designed with a clean visual style. Modern web design favors the use of text rather than buttons for menu items. When dividing information into manageable sections on a page, it is best to consider the primary mode of delivery (computer or mobile device). If learners are expected to access materials on mobile devices, be sure that information blocks are readable and scrollable.

Page layout affects white space and contrast within the pages of the course, which in turn affects accessibility and readability. Large blocks of information should be divided into manageable sections with sufficient white space around and between the blocks of text, diagrams, and tables to ensure that learners are not overloaded with information. Reducing content to smaller chunks enables learners to make better use of working memory and recall. Organizing course content into manageable sections makes it easier for learners to work through and process the information.[6] When visual complexity is increased—for example, including large blocks of text with limited white space—it contributes to increased cognitive load. This means the brain tends to work harder in order to process information.[7] Therefore, breaking down larger blocks of text into smaller chunks provides learners with a visual break and, in turn, makes it easier for them to work through the course.

Titles and headings play an important role in catching readers' interest and guiding their progress through information.[8] By using titles and headings, instructors can effectively guide learners through an online course while outlining what learners can expect along the way. In this context, readability refers to how words and blocks of text appear on a page, as well as how learners are able to scan from one item to the next. Titles and headings indicate priority and provide direction within the visual framework of a page or set of pages in an online course. This helps to structure the document and helps learners establish a flow through course content.

Hierarchy is another key element of readability. Titles and headings establish visual hierarchy and enhance the learner experience by creating a pattern or sequence through the learning content. This helps learners find their way and visually guides their progress through the content of the course.

Page design should use a consistent color scheme, avoiding red/green/ purple combinations that are hard for color blind individuals to navigate. Low contrast between text and background on computer screens and mobile devices can decrease readability and inhibit learner success in an online course.[9] Simply put, if learners are not able to easily read the course content, they may not succeed.

Low contrast leads to increased visual complexity, which makes it harder for the brain to process information.[10] Therefore, using dark text with a light-colored, neutral background is best. Sans serif fonts like Arial and Verdana are more readable online; serif fonts such as Times New Roman should be reserved for printed pages.

Course Instructions

Another element to consider in ensuring text readability in a course is clearly written instructions. When instructions are clear, learners are able to navigate the online environment without having to repeatedly ask for clarification. Instructions serve to contextualize course content, interaction, activity, and assessment by guiding learners through learning assets through the lens of the instructor.

Well-written instructions include what learners need to do, why they need to do it, and how it relates to course, module, or program objectives. Repetition of instructions throughout the course provides learners with added guidance, especially when they are associated with a specific task, activity, assignment, or assessment in the course.

Learning Modules

Assignments, activities, and discussions should be tied together with clear instructions. When materials are posted as files without much explanation, students can find it hard to follow what they are being asked to do. For example, when setting up the description of an assignment, it can be helpful to reiterate guidelines and due dates, even if this information is provided in the syllabus.

All links—whether to a website or to another document in the online classroom—should open in a new window. This will help keep learners present in the course while they are accessing the new resource. This is real help when students are trying to refer to multiple resources and access assignments and activities, because they can juggle and rearrange windows on the desktop as they see fit.

SPECIFIC ACCESSIBILITY TECHNIQUES

- Any photographic image in your course should include an alt tag to describe what's on it. Screen readers for the blind and visually impaired will read this text, making the image accessible to visually impaired learners.

- Many people with visual impairments use keyboard input and screen readers to access online content. They rely on technology that converts text into synthesized speech. In effect, the computer "reads" the text out loud for the user. Instructors should keep screen readers in mind when designing online content. Screen readers access text in a linear fashion from top to bottom, so make sure text has a natural flow, using headers to guide.

- In an online course, it is best to embed slide presentations rather than linking them. When the files are linked, any change to the linked file is updated in the destination file, but changes in an embedded file do not transfer to the destination file. This allows the instructor to control the information in the file.

- It is also best to embed videos rather than linking them. Embedding video files ensures that they are accessible with or without internet and cannot be altered by learners.

- When using videos that don't include closed-captioning, instructors can use tools to create captions. SubRip subtitle files (SRT) are plain-text files that contain subtitle information. They include start and stop times next to the subtitle text, ensuring they'll be displayed at exactly the right moment in the video. Almost any text editor—such as Notepad for Windows users and TextEdit for Mac users—may be used to create SRT files, and YouTube also offers an SRT file creator.

TIPS FOR VISUAL DESIGN AND ACCESSIBILITY

- Make sure the course is organized or structured with a main or welcome page and that other aspects of the course are easy to find from that main page.

- Include a "Welcome to the Course" page to help with orientation to the course and to create a safe trusting online environment.

- Ensure that interactive elements are easy to identify.

- Provide clear and consistent navigation options.

- Use headings and spacing to group related content.

- Include image and media alternatives in your design.

- Provide controls for content that starts automatically.

- Organize the course in modules.

- Post expectations, including grading assignment expectations, clearly and make sure they are highly visible.

- Reiterate expectations and instructions often throughout the course.

- Post a different welcome page for each module. Include new images or visuals with a slightly different welcome to each module, as well as new information to maintain student interest and involvement.

- Provide online text in a visually appealing manner with consistent font color and size to guide the learner.

- Include pictures, charts, color design, artwork, and other visuals in your welcome pages, readings, and other web pages in the online classroom.

- Include good design elements such as color, borders, clip art, and photos to increase visual interest in the content provided.

- Provide sufficient contrast between foreground and background on the screen to increase accessibility of information.

- Don't use color alone to convey information, as some learners may not distinguish color.

- Name course parts and sections consistently throughout the course.

- Provide a visual calendar of coursework and assignments.

NOTES

1. Denis Collins, James Weber, and Rebecca Zambrano, "Teaching Business Ethics Online: Perspectives on Course Design, Delivery, Student Engagement, and Assessment," *Journal of Business Ethics* 125, no. 3 (2013): 513–29. doi:10.1007/s10551-013-1932-7.

2. Arthur J. Borgemenke, William C. Holt, and Wade W. Fish, "Universal Course Shell Template Design and Implementation to Enhance Student Outcomes in Online Coursework" *Quarterly Review of Distance Education* 14, no. 1 (spring 2013): 17–23.

3. Tim J. Bristol and JoAnn Zerwekh, *Essentials of E-learning for Nurse Educators* (Philadelphia: F. A. Davis Company, 2011.

4. John Sener, "Quality Matters: Inter-institutional Quality Improvement for Online Courses," *Journal of Asynchronous Learning Networks* 10, no. 1 (2006): 69–80.

5. Ibid.

6. Mine Munyofu, William J. Swain, Bradley D. Ausman, Huifen Lin, Khusro Kidwai, and Francis Dwyer, "The Effect of Different Chunking Strategies in Complementing Animated Instruction," *Learning, Media, and Technology* 32, no. 4 (2007): 407–19. doi:10.1080/17439880701690109.

7. Simon Harper, Eleni Michailidou, and Robert Stevens, "Toward a Definition of Visual Complexity as an Implicit Measure of Cognitive Load," *ACM Transactions on Applied Perception* 6, no. 2 (2009): 1–18. doi:10.1145/1498700.1498704.

8. E. A. Lazareva, "The Headline Complex of a Text—A Means of Organizing and Optimizing Perception," *Proceedings of the Ural State University* 40 (2006): 158–66.

9. Richard E. Mayer, *The Cambridge Handbook of Multimedia Learning* (Cambridge: Cambridge University Press, 2014).

10. Harper, Michailidou, and Stevens, "Toward a Definition of Visual Complexity."

Chapter 7

Course Goals and Performance Assessments

Aligning to Course Goals and Developing Engaging Assessments

As a novice teacher, Laura Garcia's priority was her course content, and she was ready to share it with her students so they would learn to like the content as much as she did. Laura was eager to become an online instructor and had developed several activities and assignments that she believed would help her students to understand and apply the content.

Laura had some doubts, as she was not so sure that her students were fully engaged and steadily progressing in their achievement. Laura was beginning to ask herself questions such as: What do I need to assess? When should I assess? How can I assess as quickly and effectively as possible? How can I help my students increase their engagement in and responsibility for their own learning?

ESTABLISHING COURSE GOALS FOR PERFORMANCE ASSESSMENT

This chapter will guide you through four stages of effective online teaching and learning, with an emphasis on the course goals and performance assessments. The four stages look at (1) the targets associated with planning and preparation (i.e., syllabus, schedules, and standards); (2) the tools related to engagement and environment (i.e., participation, productivity, and positivity); (3) techniques that promote assessment and achievement (i.e., monitoring, measurement, and management); and (4) tips connected with facilitation and feedback (i.e., documentation and communication).

Targets

The targets associated with the first stage of effective online teaching and learning rely upon your ability to plan and prepare your course thoroughly prior to the release of your course to your students. After your course begins, you want to be ready to attend to your students' engagement and achievement. Plus, your students are anxious to know your expectations. Three primary targets are essential to the first stage of the planning and preparation of your course goals and performance assessments: the course syllabus, your schedules, and the standards.

Course Goals

Most likely your online course has a syllabus—one that was provided to you or one you wrote yourself, either as a new course or based on an established course. The course syllabus features several essential components, including the course goals and the learning objectives. Course goals are the major outcomes contextualized in terms of the academic discipline of the course within the liberal arts, fine arts, mathematics, natural sciences, social sciences, and so on.

Course goals are long-term outcomes that encompass the anticipated knowledge, skills, and dispositions the student will possess at the end of the course for which the student usually receives a letter grade ranging from A to F related to the evaluated level of overall demonstrated proficiency. The goals for a particular course are identified by the individual instructor who teaches the course, a team of instructors who teach the course, and/or the instructors of all of the courses pertaining to a particular department and/or program of study. It is beneficial for groups of instructors to collaborate on establishing course goals for all of the courses within the department or program to ensure that all expectations related to the academic discipline are included in the selection of courses, eliminating gaps and overlaps. Groups of instructors within a department or program can easily account for all of the goals by meeting together and mapping curriculum.

Learning Objectives

After the course goals for your online course have been established and added to the syllabus, you must identify the learning objectives for each of the class sessions. A semester course usually includes sixteen weeks. Your course may schedule class sessions several times each week, once per week, once every two weeks, or even less often throughout the semester. You need to be aware of the parameters set by your institution and administration as well as by the instructors within your department and/or program as you begin to schedule your class sessions.

The way the class sessions are scheduled impacts the learning objectives. Each class session should address distinct objectives as the specific knowledge, skills, and dispositions related to that session that build upon prior learning both within the program of study and throughout the course that support the course goals. Learning objectives are monitored and measured by performance assessments to be introduced throughout this chapter.

Table 7.1 shows the relationship between goals and evaluations, and between objectives and assessments.

Table 7.2 shows a 16-week semester course organized with two class sessions per week.

The Discover, Do, Discuss, Demonstrate Model is repeated throughout the semester, and the schedule can be modified as needed.

Curriculum, Instruction, and Assessments

Although the course syllabus identifies many components describing your online course, the syllabus does not constitute the course curriculum. The curriculum encompasses the course content and all the materials and various resources accessed to understand the course content. The curriculum is identified by the course goals and class session objectives, answering the question, "What is being taught and learned?"

Table 7.1. Goals Align with Evaluations; Objectives Align with Assessments

Goal 1	Objective 1 (Week 1: Class Sessions 1 & 2) = Scores
	Objective 2 (Week 2: Class Sessions 3 & 4) = Scores
	Objective 3 (Week 3: Class Sessions 5 & 6) = Score
Goal 2	Objective 4 (Week 4: Class Sessions 7 & 8) = Scores
	Objective 5 (Week 5: Class Sessions 9 & 10) = Scores
	Objective 6 (Week 6: Class Sessions 11 & 12) = Scores
Goal 3	Objective 7 (Week 7: Class Sessions 13 & 14) = Scores
	Objective 8 (Week 8: Class Sessions 15 & 16) = Scores
	Midsemester Review and Test over Goals 1, 2, and 3 = Grade
Goal 4	Objective 9 (Week 9: Class Sessions 17 & 18) = Scores
	Objective 10 (Week 10: Class Sessions 19 & 20) = Scores
	Objective 11 (Week 11: Class Sessions 21 & 22) = Scores
Goal 5	Objective 12 (Week 12: Class Sessions 23 & 24) = Scores
	Objective 13 (Week 13: Class Sessions 25 & 26) = Scores
	Objective 14 (Week 14: Class Sessions 27 & 28) = Scores
Goal 6	Objective 15 (Week 15: Class Sessions 29 & 30) = Scores
	Final Review and Test over Goals 4, 5, and 6 = Grade

Table 7.2. 16 Weeks, Two Class Sessions per Week: The Discover, Do, Discuss, Demonstrate Model

Week 1	
Session 1	Prior to Session: Read documents, listen to recordings, *discover* new information, and *do* assignment. The first draft of the assignment must be submitted prior to the start of class.
	During Session: All students must attend the class session. Instructor answers students' questions. All students are expected to ask at least one question, either prepared in advance or extending from other students' questions. Instructor scores students for their participation in the discussion and their submissions for completion, not for accuracy. Submissions are not returned.
Session 2	Prior to Session: Submit final draft of assignment.
	During Session: Students *discuss* their discoveries and *demonstrate* their products. Instructor scores students for their participation in the discussion, their demonstration of their products, and the accuracy of their submissions. Submissions are returned prior to the next class session.
Week 2	
Session 3	Repeat the two-session sequence presented for Week 1 with one addition. During session 3, the instructor provides general feedback about the previous class session's submissions and answers questions related to the previous submissions.

The instruction incorporates all of the actions taken by the instructor before, during, and after the class session. An instructor's actions may be called strategies or methods and answer the question, "How is the course curriculum being taught and learned?"

Curriculum and instruction—the *what* and *how*—must align with the assessments. Assessments answer the questions, Why are these goals and objectives being taught and learned? and, Why are these goals and objectives being taught and learned this way?

Assessments are used to monitor, measure, and manage the teaching and learning; however, the greater reason assessments are essential are to provide clarity of the purposes of the teaching and learning. The purposes of the course relate to the reason the course goals and objectives are important to understand the academic discipline, especially as part of a particular program of study.

Although most instructors begin alignment of their curriculum, instruction, and assessments by first selecting their curricular content, then selecting their instructional strategies, and finishing by selecting their assessment procedures, you are strongly encouraged to reverse this approach. Consider the outcomes that you want your students to understand as concepts and to develop as products. These outcomes are called your students' *performance* and are most likely demonstrated in your online course via writing and speaking.

ASSESSMENT STANDARDS

Becoming acquainted with the assessment standards as you select your course goals equips and empowers you to optimize your teaching and learning. The assessment standards were written by the Joint Committee on Standards for Educational Evaluation (JCSEE), which includes representatives of many different professional organizations. In 2003, members of the JCSEE defined *assessment* thus:

> Assessment is broadly defined in the Classroom Assessment Standards as the process of collecting and interpreting information that can be used to inform teachers, students, and when applicable, parents/guardians or other users' assessment information about students' progress in attaining the knowledge, skills, attitudes, and behaviors to be learned or acquired in school.[1]

The standards are divided into three broad domains: foundations, use, and quality.

Foundation assessment standards establish the basis for developing and implementing sound and fair assessment practices focused on the students being assessed. Foundation assessment standards include:

F1 Assessment Purpose
F2 Learning Expectations
F3 Assessment Design
F4 Student Engagement in Assessment
F5 Assessment Preparation
F6 Informed Students and Parents/Guardians (as appropriate)

Use assessment standards align the process and follow a logical progression from selection and development to communication of results. Use assessment standards include:

U1 Analysis of Student Performance
U2 Effective Feedback
U3 Instructional Follow-Up
U4 Grades and Summary Comments
U5 Reporting

Quality assessment standards ensure that results yield data that are accurate, reliable, bias free, and inclusive of all students, and that improve teaching and learning. Quality assessment standards include:

Q1 Cultural and Linguistic Diversity
Q2 Exceptionality and Special Education

Q3   Freedom from Bias
Q4   Validity
Q5   Reliability
Q6   Reflection

All seventeen assessment standards are critical to every online course. As you begin to align your curriculum, instruction, and assessments and match your objectives with your assessments, watch for the presence (and power) of each of these standards in the context of your academic discipline.

TOOLS FOR COURSE GOALS
AND PERFORMANCE ASSESSMENTS

The tools related to the second stage of effective online teaching and learning are key to increasing student participation, productivity, and positivity. You not only want your students to become more engaged in their learning, you want them to expand their productivity so the learning is meaningful and relevant. In addition, you should want students to enjoy the environment and their learning in ways that are both challenging and rewarding. You can accomplish these expectations through your assessments with attention to the assessment participants, the assessment cycle, and the assessment approaches. Soon will you discover that you have many options that strengthen both your teaching and your students' learning.

Assessment Participants

Assessment should be viewed as an opportunity to reflect upon progress and productivity in order to encourage engagement and advance achievement. However, most students view assessment as a pointless external threat. The word *test* tends to make many students uncomfortable, and too often students cannot explain the purpose of the test or account for their progress and the impact on their education. Therefore, you are urged to broaden the number of participants in the assessment process. The first person who should be included in the progress is the student who is being assessed. The student must be shown the way to reflect mindfully on the discussion, demonstration, and documents prepared for submission.

The second category of participant is the student peer. Peers should not provide scores or grades; peers should instead provide guidance called *peer review* using specific criteria for discussions, demonstrations, and documents prepared for submission. Although most students do not want their performance assessed by their peers, peer review is extremely important when the process is organized and communicated so the outcomes are positive and productive. All students become more attentive to their productivity when it is subjected to peer review.

The third person who is involved in the assessment process is you, the instructor. You will benefit greatly by equipping yourself with the tools and techniques shared throughout this chapter. Occasionally, in some courses or programs of study, an outsider may also be involved in the assessment process, for example, when a standardized test is required or when the student is supervised by another person as during an internship.

The Assessment Cycle

Assessment does not happen exclusively at the end of the lesson, unit of learning, or course. Assessment happens multiple times during all lessons, units of learning, and courses, as shown by the assessment cycle in figure 7.1. The assessment cycle applies both to measuring, monitoring, and managing course goals (which culminate in the overall evaluation reported as grades) and to measuring, monitoring, and managing learning objectives (which culminate in the performance assessments reported as scores).

The first stage of the assessment cycle for a course begins by administering the pre-assessment before the students have started reading, viewing, or listening to any of the course materials and resources. The pre-assessment should consist of no more than twenty-five items related to the course goals—not to

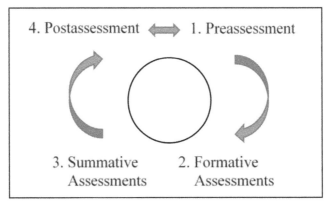

Figure 7.1. The Assessment Cycle

minutiae. Ideally you should use assessments with selected answers such as matching, multiple-choice, and true-or-false items. Selected-answer items are more challenging to develop but much easier and quicker to score objectively. With most online programs, selected answer items can be scored by the computer.

Assessments with constructed responses that involve writing words, phrases, sentences, and paragraphs are much easier and quicker to develop but much more challenging to score, and scoring of these types of questions involves subjectivity on the part of the instructor. However, students can guess the correct answers to selected-answer items without acquiring the appropriate knowledge, skills, and dispositions; students cannot guess the correct answers to constructed-response items and must support their understanding of the appropriate knowledge, skills, and dispositions.

Most of the class session activities and assignments—that is, discussions and demonstrations—constitute the formative assessments. Various formative assessments are discussed elsewhere in this chapter. Formative assessments reflect the class session objectives and related knowledge, skills, and dispositions. The major activities and assignments, including the mid-semester and final semester tests constitute the summative assessments, as the name suggests. Summative assessments reflect the accumulation of knowledge, skills, and dispositions.

The post-assessment should be the same instrument used for the pre-assessment. This is vital because it allows you to compare and contrast your students' growth from the beginning to the end of the semester. Ideally, your students should not score well on the pre-assessment and should score extremely well on the post-assessment.

You will follow the assessment cycle for each class session or sessions, depending on the way you have organized your schedule. Begin by administering a brief pre-assessment of no more than ten items. Again, selected answer items are sufficient. As you proceed through the class session, you will want to conduct a variety of formative assessments to monitor, measure, and manage progress during the discussions and demonstrations that occur while the class session is occurring and when scoring submissions.

Formative assessments can include any kind of activity or assignment using mobile apps, including, but not limited to:

- AudioNote
- Diagnoser
- DropBox
- Evernote
- ExitTicket

- Flipboard
- Glogster
- Gnowledge
- Google Docs, Drawings, Forms, Presentations, Photos, Sheets, and Slides
- Interact Quiz Builder
- Kahoot!
- Microsoft Excel Moodle
- Naiku
- Poll Everywhere
- Questbase
- Screencast-O-Matic
- Socrative
- Tell About This
- Voice Thread
- Wikispaces

You will not conduct a summative assessment for each class session; however, you should conclude the class session by re-administering the pre-assessment as a post-assessment. For units of learning or the complete course, summative assessments usually include major papers, projects, panels, PowerPoints, YouTube, tests, and other activities that summarize learning over a longer period of time.

Assessment Approaches

Only three approaches to assessment exist in most academic areas: watching, listening, and reading written products. During an online course, your students may be required to demonstrate actions that you watch using a system such as Skype, or you may require your students to submit a video such as VideoAnt. For each of these situations, you are watching a performance that you will need to be prepared to assess and score according to predetermined criteria.

Likewise, during your online course, your students may be required to talk to you, as well as talk to other students while you are listening. Again, you will need to be prepared to assess your students' spoken words according to predetermined criteria.

The most common approach to assessing students enrolled in an online course is by reading written products. When scoring written products, the criteria for the content must be established and communicated well in advance, and the criteria for appearance and quality of the product also must be established and communicated to the students.

Quick Review

At this point, you should understand that your course has a purpose established as course goals and class sessions guided by learning objectives and learning performances. Your course goals and learning objectives are specific to your academic discipline, yet all seventeen of the assessment standards must be visible and viable in your assessment that will be monitored, measured, and managed through the assessment cycle.

Assessments will be conducted as pre-assessments, formative assessments, summative assessments, and post-assessments. Post-assessments should use the same instrument as the pre-assessment. Assessments will be conducted by the student, peers, and you—the instructor—by watching, listening, and reading student work. All assessments should be based on specific criteria that are established and communicated well in advance of completion.

TECHNIQUES FOR COURSE GOALS AND PERFORMANCE ASSESSMENTS

The techniques related to the third stage of effective online teaching and learning promote assessment and achievement as you monitor, measure, and manage expectations and evidence of learning. Specifically, each of your assessments must be constructed with close attention to the clarity and communication regarding the method of expression, the complexity of thinking, and the form of documentation (i.e., checklist or rubric). Most students will produce exactly as you instruct them to, so you must focus on these three techniques with every assessment you conduct

Methods of Expression and Levels of Thinking

Assessments are composed of two components: methods of expression and levels of thinking. An assessment's *method of expression* describes the way that the assessment is worded, which determines the way students will complete it. Your assessment instructions must stipulate whether students are to select, write, show, or tell an outcome.

The wording of the assessment also determines the *level of thinking* related to the information or inquiry that the assessment is attempting to elicit from the student. Your assessment instructions could range from basic recall, to more complex logic, to integrated application, to advanced creativity, and finally, to personalized perspectives and dispositions.

Five Methods of Expression

1. *Selected Answers*: Students *pick* from a given selection or provided list (i.e., matching, multiple-choice, placing in order, true-or-false, etc.). All selected answer assessments are prepared for students to identify the correct answer by selecting one of the provided answers (i.e., circling, underlining, bubbling in a circle, drawing a box around, etc.). Selected answer assessments are challenging to writing but easy and quick to score. Selected-answer assessments allow for guessing and may not provide the best insights into students' knowledge, skills, and dispositions.

2. *Constructed Responses*: Students *write* in a variety of formats (i.e., word, phrase, sentence, fill-in-the-blank, short answer, paragraph, essay, report, etc.). All constructed responses are student generated and no word lists or other clues are provided. The opposite of selected answers, constructed responses are easy and quick to prepare but challenging to score. Constructed responses require assessment of both the content and the communication.

3. *Spoken Communication*: Students *say* what they know, formally and informally, through direct and indirect conversations using spoken words, phrases, sentences, paragraphs (i.e., giving directions, asking and/or answering questions, telling stories). Like constructed responses, all spoken communications are student generated.

   Spoken communications are frequently given in front of other students so that students build upon other spoken communications. One approach to elicit the students' own original thoughts is to ask them to write their communication before they speak. Then students can read their spoken communications aloud, verifying their original intent, and add new information that has not been reported by other students.

4. *Demonstrated Performances*: Students *show* outcomes created by and illustrated through interactions generated by the respondent (i.e., demonstrating procedures or steps, modeling, singing, acting, presenting overviews—all actions demonstrated, usually without accompanied spoken communication). Demonstrated performances can be as basic as pointing to an item or placing an object as instructed.

   Examples of demonstrated performances might also include solving a mathematical equation, drawing a map or schematic, or performing a physical task as related to physical education, dance, and so on. Scoring demonstrated responses is quite challenging and subjective; consider the panel of judges for many Olympic events.

5. *Combinations of Methods*: Eleven different combinations can be made by combining the four methods using keywords:

- pick and write
- pick and say
- pick and show
- write and say
- write and show
- say and show
- pick, write, and say
- pick, write, and show
- pick, say, and show
- write, say, and show
- pick, write, say, and show

FIVE LEVELS OF THINKING

When you assess, not only must you consider the five methods of expression, you must also attend to the five levels of thinking. Some assessments are accomplished through basic recall; other assessments require more advanced creativity. Keep in mind that your assessments will include a method of expression and a level of thinking: for example, "On the US map, point (demonstrated performance/show) to the state capital of Arkansas (recall and recognition)."

1. Recall and Recognition: these assessments ask for information related to *who, what, where, and when.*
2. Logic and Reasoning: these assessments ask for information related to *why, why not, and how do you know.*
3. Skills and Applications: these assessments ask for information related to *how do you do that, show me, and can you give me an example.*
4. Productivity and Creativity: these assessments ask for information related to *how would you make one, how does it work, and what is another or different way.*
5. Outlooks and Dispositions: these assessments ask for information related to *how do you feel, how would someone else feel, why, and why not.*

FORMS OF ASSESSMENT:
CHECKLISTS AND RUBRICS

The two most common assessment forms are checklists and rubrics. Checklists usually allow for the names of the students to be inserted in a column on the left and the desired result inserted in a row across the top, as shown in table 7.3. Checklists lend themselves well to assessing discussions and demonstrations.

Table 7.3. Sample Checklist

	Submitted First Draft	Online Full Time	Asks Question	Answers Question	Expresses Understanding	Seems Interested	Other
Ann							
Clint							
Dario							
Greg							
Laura							
LeShandra							

Score using +, ✓, or −; add comments as wanted.

Rubrics are complex checklists, as shown in table 7.4. To start, the activity/ assignment should be recorded in the top cell. You may want to include a particular goal or standard, particularly if this practice is expected by your institution.

You may want to use the 3 × 3 × 3 rubric that includes at least three levels of scores, three kinds of outcomes, and three kinds of evidence. The three levels of scores communicate to the student that everyone can score well on the activity/assignment. The three kinds of outcomes allow students to see that the activity/assignment is holistic and that all parts are valued. The three kinds of evidence can include qualitative data (i.e., evidence expressed in words and narratives for which writing content and mechanisms are scored), quantitative data (i.e., evidence accounted by a particular number associated with the evidence), and connective data (i.e., evidence personalized by the student). Connective data allows the student to become an active participant in the activity/assignment and increases the likelihood that the student will stay engaged and increase achievement.

To finish the rubric, leave a line for the student to add comments or ask questions as well as for the instructor to provide feedback.

Many different checklists and rubrics are available online. These include the Assessment Checklist Template, Canva, iRubric, Online Quiz Creator, QuickRubric, QuizStar, Rubric-Maker, and RubiStar.

Tests

When constructing a test and writing test items, be sure to review the methods of expression and levels of thinking carefully. A test should measure student progress, and from your data analysis (discussed in the next chapter), you will discover keen insights you can use to improve your course. Your test preparation must consider the conditions associated with the test taking; for example, with online courses, your students may be taking the test with other students from the course, with access to materials and resources, while on the internet, and so on.

Instructors should write test items that require students to apply their newly formed knowledge, skills, and dispositions; limit the time so that students must focus exclusively on the test; create different versions of the test so that students cannot help one another; and so forth. Alternatively, you want your test to be arranged so that students can refer to their materials and resources to create a product that extends the learning appropriately.

Table 7.4. Sample Rubric

Outcomes	High	Med	Low	Self-Assessment	Instructor Assessment
Knowledge	9–10	7–8	0–6		
Skill	9–10	7–8	0–6		
Disposition	9–10	7–8	0–6		
TOTAL					
Student comment or question					
Instructor feedback					

TIPS FOR COURSE GOALS AND
PERFORMANCE ASSESSMENTS

The assessment tips are connected with facilitation and feedback highlighting the importance of samples and support. As you plan and prepare your course, engage your students in a meaningful learning environment, and conduct assessments and to increase achievement, it is beneficial to provide your students with samples and support.

- Be flexible.
- Provide a sample:

   As you facilitate your online course, you may be asked by some students to provide more explanation or description of a particular activity or assignment. These inquiries may be raised during the class session if your online course is synchronous, or you may receive telephone calls or e-mail messages if your online course is asynchronous. You may wonder if your instructions are not clear or why some students are not sure of your expectations.

   Many students like to see a sample of the final product for an activity or assignment. By adding a sample to your online course, you help your students visualize your expectations, reduce their uncertainty and questions, and allow them to become creative by building upon the ideas you have posted for everyone to see. Additionally, by posting a sample, you can refer to it when providing assistance before the due date or when reporting feedback after you score the submission.

- Provide quality feedback:

   Quality feedback is essential for every submission. Your feedback should: (a) address the student by name; (b) identify at least one specific and perhaps unique accomplishment on the student's submission; (c) describe the parts of the submission that needed more attention, using positive and professional language that is motivating and reassuring; and (d) report the score and offer additional assistance via phone, Skype, or other means, as warranted.

   Writing quality feedback can be tricky. Although you may dedicate time and energy to writing narratives to guide and support your students, most students will be more focused on their numerical scores. Students certainly remember grades if you choose to use them on your formative assessments. You may want to use numerical scores throughout your course and assign letter grades only when the course has ended.

- PACE yourself:

    The targets, tools, and techniques in this chapter focus on the assessment process, which begins with the establishment of course goals and ends with the collection of data documented by performance assessments. This assessment process can be summarized with the acronym PACE—Purpose, Alignment, Cycle, and Evidence.

    As the instructor of an online course, you must be both mindful and intentional about the purpose of your course so you can evaluate your students fairly at the end of course. Your purpose is reinforced by the goals that frame the holistic nature of the course and the objectives that guide each learning experience or class sessions.

NOTE

1. Joint Committee on Standards for the Evaluation of Education, Classroom Assessment Standards: Sound Assessment Practices for PK–12 Teachers (2003): http://www.jcsee.org/the-classroom-assessment-standards-new-standards.

Chapter 8

Data Analysis and Course Improvement

Recording Outcomes, Analyzing Data, and Interpreting Findings

In his online course, Craig Erics follows the assessment cycle and conducts pre-assessments, formative assessments, summative assessments, and post-assessments for his units of learning and within his daily lesson plans. Although he records great amounts of data, Craig is unsure of what the next steps should be in terms of looking at the data. Meanwhile, his students continue to demonstrate the same outcomes, some of which are mediocre, so Craig realizes that he needs to modify his course. Craig wants to use the data he has collected to increase his students' engagement and achievement, and, most importantly, to make changes to improve his course and ultimately his efficacy and agency.

Building on the previous chapter, this chapter will guide you through the procedures for analyzing data and improving your course. The targets of this chapter focus on the purposes, perspectives, and pre/post-assessment principles associated with data analysis and course improvement. The tools provided in this chapter delve into the ways to record, analyze, and interpret findings. The techniques discussed in this chapter identify six parts of content organization and five parts of online presence for which you should ask for feedback. Finally, the tips in this chapter review the importance of ethics and efficacy in your assessments, analysis, and accountability for improving your online course.

TARGETS

Three targets dominate this chapter: the purposes, the perspectives, and the pre/post-assessment principles associated with data analysis and course improvement. The purposes of data analysis are more complex than most instructors understand in concept and/or apply to their practices.

Becoming acquainted with the purposes of data analysis establishes a firm foundation for embarking upon the next steps and vital benefits associated with course improvement. Data analysis requires instructors to consider outcomes from multiple perspectives that they may not have previously recognized or with which they are comfortable. Many instructors do not consider their learners as active participants—much less as partners—in teaching, learning, and schooling. Considering multiple perspectives is critical, enlightens interconnectedness, and verifies their influence on the success and satisfaction of everyone involved.

Purposes of Analyzing Data

Data analysis begins only after you have conducted your assessments and documented your data, as described in the previous chapter. The purpose of analysis requires that you view your work from three critical, interconnected, and influential perspectives, as shown in figure 8.1. The three perspectives are teaching, learning, and schooling, which function both separately and collectively as one entity. *Teaching* incorporates all the actions of the instructor; *learning* incorporates all the actions of the students; and *schooling* incorporates all the policies, programs, procedures, materials, resources, and so on of the institution, especially items over which the teacher and students have little or no control. Each of the three perspectives is critical for the other two perspectives to exist; collectively, the three perspectives function simultaneously, relying on the interconnectivity and responding to the influences among the three perspectives, with assessments, analysis, and accountability at the center.

The teacher is responsible for preparing and conducting assessments following the guidelines provided throughout this book according to the standards and expectations established by the institution and contextualized to a particular age group, grade level, academic subject area, program of study, degree program, and so on. Concomitantly, the teacher is responsible for analyzing data and improving the course to increase student engagement and achievement while enhancing teacher efficacy and agency.

Efficacy encompasses the teacher's sense of responsibility and degree of ability to increase student learning, while *agency* encompasses the teacher's sense of ownership and degree of dedication to ensure the increase in student learning occurs. Teaching, learning, and schooling are collectively focused on the three *A*'s: assessments, analysis, and accountability. *Assessments* collect the data; *analysis* reveals insights into strengths and weaknesses; and

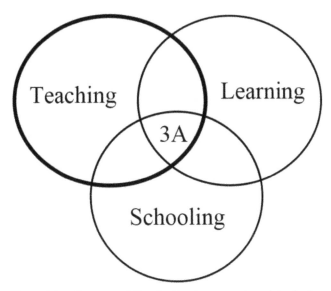

Figure 8.1. Purposes of Conducting Assessments and Analyzing Data

accountability prompts instructors to enhance their efficacy and agency for themselves, to their students, and within their institutions.

Perspectives

When analyzing data, you must view the assessment data from each perspective. From the perspective of teaching, ask yourself if your identified methods of expression, levels of thinking, and forms of assessments are the most appropriate and whether you communicated your expectations clearly and concisely. Your data analysis must consider the teacher's effectiveness to align the assessment with the goal so that the data tell the anticipated story aligned with your curriculum and instruction.

From the perspective of learning, ask yourself if all parts of your assessment allowed the students to understand the expectations and provided them with opportunities to excel. In particular, were students given choices in their assessments, options to individualize their outcomes, and ways to make individual connections? You not only want your students to demonstrate their proficiency with the immediate information, you also want to provide opportunities for students to communicate and connect with continuing concepts and lifelong learning and living.

From the perspective of schooling, ask yourself if the assessment supports the policy and programs of the institution and contributes to the mission, vision, and values of the institution. Here the term *institution* also includes the grade level, department, team, program, or degree relevant to your students and course.

The purpose of data analysis must be visible in each of the three entities, as each of the three entities participate in the process.

Simultaneously, your data analysis must be considered holistically as a meta-cognitive experience. You will find it beneficial to consider your data analysis as a unifying thread that runs through the entire procedure as you plan, facilitate, and inspect both the assessments and the analysis from the three perspectives.

You need the assessment and analysis procedures collectively to help you recognize your own perspectives, including your policies, practices, and possibly your patterns and prejudices. You need to be attuned to your patterns, not only for preparing and conducting assessments but also for analyzing your data and modifying your procedures. Look for the ways you communicate your expectations, guide your students through the concepts and practices, prepare them for assessments, invite them into the assessment procedures, include them in the data analysis, and solicit suggestions regarding course improvements.

You should also be aware of your own prejudices. Do you prepare all of your students for all assessment items in ways that are fair and objective? Do you conduct your assessments to enhance success for all students? Do you analyze data to show reasonable and impartial expectations?

Keep in mind that you want to transform your students' metacognitive beliefs and behaviors associated with the overall assessment process and analysis procedures as related to both short-term results and long-term ramifications. Consider adding opportunities for students to delve into their short-term and long-term discoveries and share outcomes with peers via think-pair-share reflections, one-minute stream-of-consciousness papers, concept mapping and graphic organizers, and assessment wrapping for students to examine their strengths and weaknesses on various assessments.

Remember that the overall goal of your course is to connect learning with living; your students will benefit when you lead these exercises and prompt their thinking about thinking. Ask your students to communicate their own analyses with you as the teacher so you can consider them when making course improvements.

Pre/Post-Assessment Principles

Although it sounds logical that in order to analyze data, you must collect data, far too many instructors collect only post-assessment data. Collecting only post-assessment data does not equip or empower you with any insights about teaching, learning, or schooling; it merely provides you with post-assessment data (most likely a test) and scores that cannot be analyzed or contribute to your accountability.

The assessment cycle discussed in chapter 7 illustrates four assessments used to collect data: pre-assessments, formative assessments, summative assessments, and post-assessments. At the beginning of a course of study or a unit of learning, you must collect pre-assessment data before the teaching, learning, and schooling begin so that you can compare and contrast the initial knowledge, skills, and dispositions with those documented in the post-assessment data.

Likewise, at the beginning of a lesson you must conduct a pre-assessment so you can compare and contrast the data with the post-assessment data. This assessment and analysis principle is essential for you to acquire insights into your students' proficiencies and your own practices.

TOOLS

In order to record outcomes, analyze data, and interpret findings, you must be ready with the equipment and the enthusiasm to explore your current routines and tools and consider new ones. While various tools have been shared with you throughout this book, keep in mind that new tools are becoming available at all times, and current tools quickly become outdated. You also need to be attuned to the tools that your institution offers and/or expects you to use. Frequently, your institution's information technology support will help you only with tools offered by the institution.

Your students have developed deeply held beliefs and firmly established behaviors regarding assessments and analysis from many years of interactions—primarily one-way—with their various teachers. Students tend to see themselves as recipients of the teacher's plans and procedures; rarely are students considered participants, much less partners, in teaching, learning, and schooling.

You should try to provide opportunities for your students to tailor the demonstration of their outcomes to their own needs and interests by giving them voice and choice in the assessment tools. Ideally, your assessments and analyses should spark conversations among your students, not just to improve their scores but also to increase their participation in the course and connections to both their learning and living.

Record Outcomes

The most efficient way to analyze data is to create an Excel spreadsheet, or a series of spreadsheets, with your students' names inserted into the first column on the left. You may want to avoid using names (to increase ethics and reduce any risk of bias) by replacing each student's name with a numerical code. If you replace your students' names with numerical codes, be sure to reorganize the list so the students' codes do not correspond to their names in the order in which their names are listed on your online course roster.

In the second column on the spreadsheet, insert each student's pre-assessment score. Then, when the time arrives, in the third column on the spreadsheet, insert the post-assessment scores. The functions of Excel allow you to quickly calculate the change in each student's score.

On another spreadsheet—again using the students' names or codes in the left-hand column—create a column for each of the pre-assessment items. For example, if your pre-assessment includes twenty items, then you will use twenty columns. For each student, place a "0" in the column if the student did not answer the item correctly and 1 in the column if the student did answer the item correctly. When you have inserted all data, you can use the Excel spreadsheet functions to calculate (a) the total number of items that each student answered correctly and (b) the total number of students who answered each item correctly, as shown in figures 8.2 and 8.3. The functions of the Excel spreadsheet allow you to create graphs so you can visualize the data easily.

Analyze Data

By looking at the graph showing the total number of items the students answered correctly, you can identify the students who did and who did not score well on the pre-assessment. For the high scores, however, you

Figure 8.2. Post-Assessment by Student Code

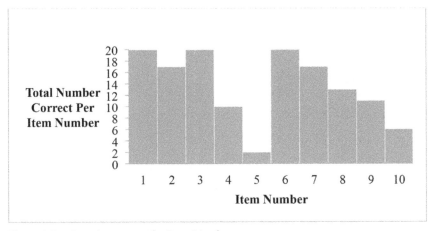

Figure 8.3. Post-Assessment by Item Number

do not know if students actually knew the information, guessed well on the multiple-choice items, used outside materials or other individuals to help them, and so on. For the low scores, you do not know if students did not understand the item, misread the item, ran out of time, experienced an electronic challenge, or the like.

To gain more insight into your pre/post-assessment items, you can create another spreadsheet with all of those possible answers for each of your items. For example, if item number 1 has four possible answers, then create a column for 1a, 1b, 1c, and 1d. Continue this procedure until you have listed all of the possible answers for all of the items.

Using the Excel spreadsheet functions, you can create graphs illustrating the answers given by each student and the answers given for each item. This visualization is extremely helpful for pre/post-assessment because you can compare and contrast the specific changes in the students' answers from the beginning to the end of the semester, as shown in figure 8.4. Keep in mind that you should not change your post-assessment items after you have administered the pre-assessment; you want the items to remain the same from the beginning to the end of the course. You can change the items the next time you teach the online course.

Interpret Findings

When looking at the graphs, you will begin to notice trends that are evident by student and trends that are evident by item. When you notice trends with individual students experiencing challenges, you should initiate intervention

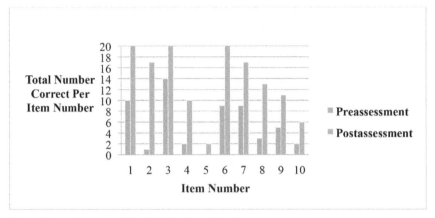

Figure 8.4.   Assessment Analysis by Item Number

to assist the student. When student trends are shared by a group of students, you want to consider various situations:

- Did these students miss important information earlier in this course or information that should have been learned in a prerequisite course?
- Are these students misunderstanding your instructions? Perhaps they study together and the group would benefit from your assistance.
- Are your instructions written in ways that are culturally competent, using language that is easily understood by and respectful of all students?

Students are not expected to score well on a pre-assessment. Ideally, throughout the course, the information on the pre-assessment will be introduced, applied, practiced, and reviewed frequently so that students acquire the understanding necessary to score well on the post-assessment. If trends involving specific items are evident on both the pre-assessment and post-assessment, then you need to revisit the items and the presence of the concept throughout the course.

TECHNIQUES

Your online course involves many parts, and all of them impact your students' assessments. Figure 8.5 shows six parts of course organization that you must examine and constantly change to improve your course.

Curricular Content

Your curricular content includes what you teach and should align directly with your course goals. Some curricular content is taught directly and some

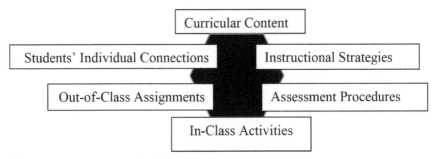

Figure 8.5. Course Organization

curricular content is taught indirectly by integration with other curricular content. You must be sure that your course goals are introduced, applied, practiced, and reviewed in detail, perhaps several times in various ways.

As you analyze data, look for gaps and overlaps related to your curricular content, especially in application to your course goals and performance assessments. When students do not complete activities or assignments as well as you anticipated, you most likely need to provide more and/or different information in your readings or recordings and connect more links to materials and resources.

Additionally, you may need to modify the order of information delivered throughout the course or during a particular class session. Course curriculum should change over time in order to keep the course current and captivating.

Instructional Strategies

Your instructional strategies incorporate how you teach and should align with your curricular content. You want to create a balance between establishing a comfortable routine and carving a boring rut in your course. Students like to become familiar with their online courses and instructors as quickly as possible. Some institutions expect their instructors to use similar formats for their online courses to aid this familiarity. However, you should not allow your routines to carve a rut.

Students also want online instructors who personalize their courses, expect students to participate in discussions and get to know one another, and encourage students to be creative in their productivity. As discussed throughout this book, many different instructional strategies exist, and many more are becoming available within various online course platforms. You are encouraged to seek professional development from national, state, and local professional associations in your academic curricular area.

Assessment Procedures

The previous chapters have acquainted you with assessment standards, the importance of course goals, and many aspects of performance assessments, including the four times to assess, as shown in the assessment cycle; the three people who should participate in assessments; and the three approaches to conducting assessments (watching, listening, and reading written products). In chapter 7 you were introduced to methods of expression, levels of thinking, and forms of assessment.

Just as with your instructional strategies, your assessment procedures need to be balanced so your students can demonstrate their proficiencies with competence and confidence. Your assessment procedures should be understandable and user-friendly; however, if and when you expect your students to expand their outcomes beyond the current materials and resources, you are strongly urged to include at least one activity or assignment previewing the expectation you have for your students to help them understand the expectations and outcomes.

In-Class Activities

Online courses—both synchronous and asynchronous—offer many different ways to help your students participate in in-class activities. In synchronous courses, you or one of your students can lead conversations on the discussion board provided by the online course platform or using other course conversation tools such as AudioNote, Google Forms, Poll Everywhere, Screencast-O-Matic, and Tell About This. In asynchronous courses, conversations can be conducted on the discussion board or the course blog. In-class activities can also include demonstrations using Flipboard; Glogster; Google Drawings, Forms, Presentations, and Slides; and LiveBinders. Online course instructors tend to modify their in-class activities frequently to improve their courses, as the tools and techniques available are constantly being refined.

Out-of-Class Assignments

In addition to in-class activities, you will also give your students out-of-class assignments related to the academic content area. These assignments may include a variety of writing tasks, projects, PowerPoint presentations, and so on. While you may presume that students can easily work on group assignments using Google Docs, be aware that some students live in remote areas where internet access is limited. In addition, students' schedules may not allow them to meet online at the same time as the other members of their groups. Group assignments must be scored carefully. Use a detailed rubric and allow each member of the group to self-assess and peer-assess so that you are provided the appropriate information when you assess both individual and group proficiency.

Out-of-class assignments will include your formative and summative assessments. For these assignments, analyze the data closely to identify any aspects of the assignments or the assessments that need to be changed to improve the course.

Students' Individual Connections

Your online course must offer your students two important opportunities to make an individual connection to the purpose of the course: voice and choice. *Voice* is the opportunity for students to personalize in-class activities or out-of-class assignments to individual interests. *Choice* is the opportunity for students to select the way in which they will demonstrate the outcomes.

For both voice and choice, you can provide your students with a list of possibilities from which they are expected to make individual connections. You can also provide your students with the list and allow them to add more suggestions that you can approve as the activity or assignment begins. Providing voice and choice for students helps them identify the course content and apply it to their lives.

PERFORMANCE-BASED ASSESSMENTS (A–Z)

Many of the following performance-based assessments can be used for pre/post-assessments, formative assessments, and/or summative assessments:[1]

- acrostics, advertisements, advice columns, agendas, animated stories, artifact replicas, artwork
- blogs, blueprints, bookmarks, books, brochures, bulletin boards, bumper stickers, business cards
- calendars, cartoons, collages, children's and young people's books, collections, commercials, constitutions, crossword puzzles
- dances, databases, debates, demonstrations, designs, diaries, directions, dioramas, documentaries, drawings
- editorials, eulogies, experiments
- fashion shows, files, fishbowl discussions, folders, foreign language words
- games, graphic organizers

- help-wanted ads, historical portrayals of persons or events
- illustrated time lines, infomercials, internet messages, internet searches, interviews, inventions, inventories
- job applications, jokes, journal entries, journeys
- K-W-L and K-W-H-L charts
- legislative hearings, letters, learning logs, license plates
- maps, menus, mobiles, mock trials, models, museums, musical compositions, musical presentations, musical scores
- newscasts, notebooks
- obituaries, oral histories, oral readings
- pantomimes, photographic essays, pictures, plans, plays, podcasts, poems, political cartoons, posters, PowerPoints, problem solutions, problems, puppet shows
- questions, questionnaires (with analyses of results), quilts
- radio shows, readers' theaters, recipes, role-playing activities
- scale models, scientific reports, scrapbook pages, scripts, signs, simulations, slideshows, songs, speeches, steps to follow, storyboards, stories, story illustrations, surveys
- t-shirts, television programs, time capsules, think-alouds, toys, travel brochures, tiered time lines, treaties
- unit summaries with illustrations
- video documentaries, virtual field trips
- websites, wikis, word banks, word walls
- xylographs (wood engravings) and other artistic renderings
- yearbooks or similar documentaries
- Z-to-A or A-to-A alphabet-type lists

Quick Check

Table 8.1 presents ten key questions to guide you with your data analysis.

In addition to improvements to your curricular content, instructional strategies, assessment procedures, in-class activities, out-of-class assignments, and students' individualized connections, you must be attentive to improvements to your online presence. You will want to ask for student comments, peer reviews, program coordinator guidance, mentor advice, and information technology support in addition to professional development from various resources.

Student Comments

Most of your students will be eager to share comments about your online course with you if the comments are anonymous and will not affect their

Table 8.1.   Key Questions when Analyzing Classroom Assessment Data

When analyzing your data:

1. What content standards were assessed?
2. What content standards were not assessed and why not?
3. What were the levels and indicators of learner proficiency?
4. What percent of learners demonstrated each level and indicator of proficiency?
5. What are the levels of proficiency by subgroups?
6. What modifications should the instructor make to increase learner engagement and achievement? (The teacher should consider the curricular content, instructional strategies, assessment procedures, in-class activities, and out-of-class assignments.)
7. After modifications, what percent of learners demonstrated each level and indictor of proficiency?
8. Did modifications or other interventions improve learner performance?
9. What modifications need to occur in the next unit of learning?
10. What modifications need to occur in the general approaches and attitudes of the teaching, learning, and schooling?

final grades. You can write questions to distribute via a survey tool such as a Google Form or SurveyMonkey. Your questions can include a Likert scale that allows students to rate specific criteria as a 5, 4, 3, 2, or 1.

The Likert scale questions could be followed by an opportunity for open response that allows students to explain their rating. You may want to ask a colleague to conduct this survey and give you the results so students are assured that you cannot trace their ratings and comments to them. If you ask students for their comments, be sure to analyze the data carefully and then make improvements to the course that you can then bring to your students' attention as being the result of their comments.

Peer Reviews

You can follow the same procedure to conduct a peer review of your online course. However, in this case the peer is not enrolled in the course and will be limited in comprehending every part of it. You may want to identify specific parts of the course for a peer or group of peers to review. You may want to ask a peer or group of peers who do not otherwise evaluate you.

Program Coordinator Guidance

Most online courses are part of a particular program, and most programs have coordinators. You can ask your program coordinator for guidance about your online course presence. Your program coordinator may not be familiar with your online course, so just as with your peers, you may want to identify specific parts of the course that you would like your program coordinator to consider.

Mentor Advice

Many instructors have mentors. A *mentor* is a peer the instructor has asked to coach him or her with teaching and other professional responsibilities. You may want to ask your mentor for advice regarding specific challenges with your online teaching or learning; alternatively, your mentor may be able to recommend another individual who can help you. Your mentor will understand you in the context of your overall growth and can coordinate the next steps holistically.

Information Technology and Online Course Support

You most likely have access to an office of information technology and online course support. The individuals associated with these services usually offer expertise ranging from answering isolated questions to providing you with detailed assistance. You may discover that one individual in particular associated with these services at your institution understands your needs and interests and resonates with your teaching goals and learning styles; this person may be an ideal partner to help you with your online course.

Professional Development

Professional development with online teaching and learning is quickly becoming more available and more focused on specific topics and issues. Most institutions provide professional development or access to professional development within the state or region. Likewise, most academic organizations offer professional development for online instructors tailored to the mission, vision, and values of the organization.

Take advantage of professional development when it is available near you. During these workshops you will discover other online course instructors, some of whom share your same level of expertise. Most likely, you will find peers with whom you can network and exchange ideas and inspiration.

TIPS

Two overarching tips applicable to both the previous chapter as well as this one relate to ethics and efficacy. Ethics are guided by your moral compass, ensuring that all your actions as an instructor are fair and equitable for all students:

Do no harm.
- Do no harm means that as an online course instructor, you should try to anticipate all potential outcomes extending from your actions and to make sound judgments from the perspective of each student.
- While this charge is impossible, you need to be cognizant that assessments may cause a range of unanticipated consequences. Your discussion prompts and test items may be confusing, tricky, unrelated, silly, sarcastic, and/or punitive.
- Ask a friend not involved in your academic field to attempt answering your discussion prompts and test items to check for unintended consequences.

Avoid score pollution.
- Avoiding score pollution involves maintaining consistency, dependability, reliability, and validity in your assessment items and data analysis practices. Assessment scores tend to become polluted when items not related to demonstrating proficiency are included with the score.
- Score pollution may appear as sneaky, unfair, unkind, and deceptive, such as when an instructor gives a pop quiz on a day when many students are absent, when an instructor changes the assessment procedure after the activity or assignment has been started, when an instructor includes behaviors not related to the activity or assignment in the score, and so on.

Communicate expectations.
- In your online course, you want to be sure that you communicate your expectations related to dates and expectations, minimize changes and/or contact each student individually when changes must be made, and be clear about the assessment criteria.
- Just as you asked a peer to attempt answering your discussion prompts or taking your test, ask a peer to restate your activity and/or assignment instructions to you based on your assessment procedures. You may discover that the instructions you believed to be clear in your own mind are not so clear in your students' minds.

Maintain efficacy.
- Data analysis and course improvements reflect your efficacy or your level of understanding and degree of commitment to the accountability of the teaching, learning, and schooling in your online course.
- After collecting the data on your students' pre-assessments, formative assessments, summative assessments, and post-assessments, it is your responsibility to review the curriculum, instructions, assessments, in-class activities, out-of-class assignments, and students' individual connections.

- Look for clarity in communications, samples of outcomes, encouragement for success, opportunity for expression and exchange of outcomes, and usefulness of feedback.
- Keep in mind that *if you continue to do what you always do, you will continue to get what you always get.*

Stay ALERT.
- The best way to optimize your students' learning is to stay ALERT, an acronym representing the awareness, learners, effectiveness, relevance, and transformation.
- Awareness: Although it is easy to become complacent with your online course, especially if your course seems to work well with one group of students, you are strongly advised to maintain a keen awareness of all parts of your course influenced by your assessments.
- Learners: Look at your course from the viewpoints of your learners; when they read your instructions, do they understand your intentions clearly, concisely, and completely?
- Effectiveness: Your course needs to be effective as part of a course of study to prepare your students for another course, college, career, community, and civic life. You are responsible for creating a course that serves as this stepping stone in your students' journeys; therefore, not only must your course be effective, *you* must be effective.
- Relevance: All parts of your course—curricular content, instructional strategies, assessment procedures, in-class activities, out-of-class assignments, and students' individual connections—need to be relevant. You must review, redo, and renew all parts of your course every time you begin again. As discussed earlier, it can be helpful to ask your students, colleagues, administrators, and mentors to provide you feedback on your online course so you can stay alert.
- Transformation: Finally, acknowledge that online teaching and learning has become a well-established platform of education as documented by the guidelines provided you in this book; however, you must balance the responsibilities, especially related to assessments, to fully appreciate and enjoy the transformation.

You want your course (and yourself) to be viewed as honest, natural, authentic, and holistic. No time is wasted in your course; students are given opportunities to connect the learning to their lives; your guidance and feedback are timely, meaningful, and supportive; and your course flows purposefully from session to session with curriculum, instruction, assessments, in-class activities, out-of-class assignments, and individual connections building upon prior experiences and outcomes to enhance student thinking, application, and creativity.

NOTES

1. Nancy P. Gallavan, *Developing Performance-Based Assessments* (Thousand Oaks, CA: Corwin Press, 2009), 128.

About the Authors

Mike Casey, MSE, instructor of management information systems in the College of Business at the University of Central Arkansas, has research interest in information and data quality, business application of statistics, online course development, and online teaching. Throughout his career he has taught mathematics and computer science in secondary and postsecondary institutions, both online and face-to-face. He has also worked as an instructional designer focusing on the development and delivery of online courses.

Erin Shaw is a visiting professor for the Department of Leadership Studies at the University of Central Arkansas and an adjunct faculty member for the Instructional Design and Technology Department at the University of Memphis, where she earned her EdD in Instructional Design and Technology. She served in K–12 education for twenty-four years and has also been an online instructor at UCA for four years. Research interests include information literacy skill instruction, online teaching, and integration of technology into the classroom. Erin is National Board certified and received the AAIM School Library Media Specialist of the Year award in 2014.

Jeff L. Whittingham, PhD, professor of teacher education in the Department of Teaching and Learning at the University of Central Arkansas, has research interest in online teaching, literacy, and educational technology. He spent thirteen years in K–12 education and is completing his sixteenth year in higher education. He has numerous peer-reviewed publications and was the lead editor of *Technological Tools in the Literacy Classroom*.

Nancy P. Gallavan, PhD, professor of teacher education in the Department of Teaching and Learning at the University of Central Arkansas, specializes in classroom assessments, cultural competence, social studies education, and internship supervision in UCA's nationally recognized MAT program. With twenty years of experience in K–12 education, twenty-five years of experience in higher education, and approximately 200 peer-reviewed publications across her areas of expertise, Nancy has received awards for teaching, service, and scholarship. Notably, Nancy served as the 2013–2014 ATE president and was honored as a 2013 KDP Eleanor Roosevelt Legacy Chapter inaugural member and a 2016 ATE Distinguished Member.